My Greece: Mirrors & Metamorphoses

Discover Each Journey as Sacred Destiny

My Greece: Mirrors & Metamorphoses
Discover Each Journey as Sacred Destiny

by Ambika Talwar
Complete Draft – Original Work / Sole Author

Email: luminousfields@gmail.com

Website: http://creativeinfinities.com
http://goldenmatrixvisions.com
http://intuition2wellness.com

ISBN: 978-1-937207-23-6

Published by Golden Matrix Visions
Creating Calm Network Publishing Group

Printed by CreateSpace, an Amazon.com company
Available on Amazon.com and other retail outlets

Cover Design by Ambika Talwar
Front and back cover photos courtesy of pixabay.com
Photo of author courtesy: Photo Hatem ~ (714) 260-1400

Reviews

"At the beginning of this surprising memoir filled with heart, humor, wonderment, and sensuality, Grandmother Melpomene (beauteous, mercurial, 97, and Greek) reads Ambika Talwar's morning coffee grounds and pronounces, "You have a long journey ahead of you. A very long journey." You will not merely read about this journey. You will be swept away as Ambika's fortunate companion on an odyssey through what she calls the "cosmic weave" between clashing cultures and shared experiences.

Oppressive heat, sumptuous food, raucous dances, and pageantry fill the entries of this astonishing work as our author visits major landmarks, humble villages, and scenic islands, often gleaning the greatest insights into the human condition well away from storied attractions and festive tavernas.

Greece is the birthplace of drama, and the drama of Ambika's travels runs the gamut from death and criminality to the celebration of new life and encounters with the two most beloved of any writer's muses: truth and beauty.

The rest still exhales as completely true for me about the book, Ambika. I'm very proud of your work in it. And always, very, very proud of you.

Part travel diary, part meditation on storytelling, heroic destinies, passion, and ancient divinity, *My Greece: Mirrors & Metamorphoses* calls on us to witness how our tales overlap, how land becomes memory, how people reveal their shadow selves, and how one gifted observer with an eye for the revealing and ravishing detail and a heart open to adventure can take us to places on Earth and in our psyches that we have never seen before."

~ Amélie Frank (Renowned Poet, publisher, Beyond Baroque board member — Los Angeles, California)

"Ambika, what I like in this piece very much is your narrative power, takes me along with you; there are passages of immediate description, complexities of relationship, wide-ranging thought, and some powerful fiction writing, vividly realised and suggestive. I thoroughly enjoyed how you evoke the people and know I will remember scenes and individuals and I like very much your presentation of the ancient and modern in Greek culture on many levels - all in all a powerful evocation of what it is to be a traveler in many dimensions, fans how that shifts in space and time and in the heart."

~ George Jisho Robertson (Poet, Buddhist priest, former English teacher — London, UK)

"Some journeys are both external and internal. Such is the case with Ambika Talwar's sensually-told tale. Her travels in Greece expose us to a keenly perceptive woman's understanding of creativity, the arts, and life and death. Initially setting out to join a screenwriting workshop, Talwar finds herself becoming part of a community. She attends a funeral, a christening, a wedding... and in her travels and relationships, finds those parts of herself that had too often been buried in day-to-day activities back home in L.A. This travel memoir through Crete, Athens, Santorini, and Delphi is interspersed with Talwar's lovely poems, visions, and dreams. As the author writes, "Making art is a journey. Taking a journey is an art." With this beautiful and sensitive book, she has made art from her journey as well."

~ Donna Baier Stein, (Author/Publisher *Tiferet* — Kansas City, Missouri)

"In *My Greece: Mirrors and Metamorphoses*, Ambika Talwar's rovings and reflections act as a guide through consciousness itself, reminding us who we are both independently and collectively. Reflecting on *The Odyssey*, various films in her screenwriting program, myths, religious tales, her own unexpected and enlightening experiences in Greece, and much more, Talwar beautifully illustrates that, "Each person is a rich magnificent story." Talwar's physical journey abounds with the sensual details of place: plates of Greek salad "peppered with feta and olives," delicious swims in the ocean, bottles of cognac waiting on tables near cemetery walls. Yet, what she ultimately helps us to realize is that the greatest journey is the one we make into ourselves and towards others—that the truth of it all, the nostalgia that drives us abroad and back home—is that "We are related ... from a long time ago."

~ Melissa Studdard (Author of *Six Weeks to Yehidah* and host of *Tiferet Talk,* English professor at Lone Star College-Tomball — Houston, Texas)

"Ambika Talwar leads us on a journey of profound wonder, of mythos and pathos, traveling through the byways of modern and ancient Greece, encountering out-of-this-world human beings who step out of mystery into light, laughter, sorrow, and high play. She weaves a tapestry centered on the feminine quest for wisdom and meaning with poetry conjured from a cauldron of energy, imagery and high magic. Her work enchants at every level."

~ Peggy Rubin, (CEO of *Sacred Theater*, Seminar leader, Change Agent — Ashland, Oregon)

"In the many ways to tell a travel story, Ambika's touches the heart, going beyond descriptions of people and places to search for the soul of Greece, which is also a journey to the inner self. This is the wonder of a tale that also finds its purest deepest expression in the weave of stories and poems that bring to life shades of this ancient land and our humanity."

~ Richard Alexander (musician, landscape artist, literature lover — Los Angeles, California)

"*My Greece* is a gentle journey into the heart and soul of what it means to be human. Ambika Talwar beautifully describes the intimate details of her travels in Greece – the sites and people she meets – in a way that invites us to take each step with her. Once comfortable with Ambika, she skillfully weaves in reflections of modern and ancient life from the perspective of an artist searching for meaning. Her depth of awareness and unassuming wisdom allows for a gradual opening of the heart as she introduces questions that, if embraced, can deepen our experience of being human."

~ Philip M. Hellmich, (Director of Peace – The Shift Network. Author of *God and Conflict* — Berkeley, California)

Acknowledgements

I am most grateful for the support and encouragement of all those who read my manuscript and commented: Donna Baier Stein, George Jisho Robertson, Melissa Studdard, Amélie Frank, Peggy Rubin, Phillip M. Hellmich, and Richard Alexander whose encouraging remarks goaded me forward at every step.

I am also grateful to Harry Altoff for his careful attention to details as he proofread and offered editorial comments while also writing and studying for a career in education. I thank Richard Alexander, musician/landscape architect, for his incisive feedback and Susan Rogers for her willingly sharing of light always in my time of distress and for reframing my moments of indecision. I thank Sophia Pandeya for her timely assistance in working with me on the stanza in the dedication.

I thank also Marianthi Constantinu for her nostalgia and her feedback. I thank all the people I met while traveling through Greece for sharing their stories, wisdom, and playfulness with me. I thank them for the inspirations that sparked poems, stories, and meditations.

Most importantly, I thank from the fullness of my being a friend who is a magnificent scholar, seer, sage, creative visionary whose deep love for wisdom and world harmony are a gift the world does not recognize, as it should. My friend has taught me so very much and has been a guide in profound ways that I cannot yet fathom. I am deeply sincerely beholden for his recognition of my specific talents and encouragement of my vision. Indeed, we both wish the world would understand the greater commonalities inherent in all our ways, rather than differences, which are created to cause separations.

I extend also my gratitude to Kimberly Burnham for taking on the risky task of preparing this book for publication, which involves much skill and concentration. This task also requires tremendous patience and an eye to detail. Kimberly showed time and again her dedication to the project, making sure I was happy with it all. A fine fellow poet, Kimberly is co-owner of Creating Calm Network Publishing Group in Spokane, WA.

My Greece: Mirrors & Metamorphoses

Discover Each Journey as Sacred Destiny

by
Ambika Talwar

Vakambhrini rishi says...

10.125.15

अहमेव वात इव पर वाम्यारभमाणा भुवनानि विश्वा ।

ahameva vāta iva pra vāmyārabhamāṇā
bhuvanāni viśvā |

*I breathe a strong breath like the wind and tempest,
while I hold together all existence.*

10.125.16

परो दिवा पर एना पर्थिव्यैतावती महिना सं बभूव ॥

paro divā para enā pṛthivyaitāvatī
mahinā saṃ babhūva ||

*Beyond this wide earth and beyond the heavens,
I have become so mighty in my grandeur.*

Vakambhrini was one of the earliest women seers and poets of all time. Her poetic utterance appears in the *RigVeda*, scripture of early India.

May we travel with her words in our heart of hearts and realize our sacred destiny as one with all existence.

http://www.ancientvedas.com/chapter/10/book/125/

Table of Contents

Reviews	3
Acknowledgements	7
Preface	11
A Dedication	15
Vakambhrini rishi says...	17
Introduction	21
Chapter 1 ~ Arrivals	27
Chapter 2 ~ Departures	41
Chapter 3 ~ In Search of Stories	49
Chapter 4 ~ Art, Life, & Alchemy	73
Chapter 5 ~ Discovering Delphi and "Ekfrastikotita"	89
Chapter 6 ~ Friezes in the Sun... Discoveries	105
Chapter 7 ~ Weave of Our Mythologies	119
Chapter 8 ~ Relationships That Reveal	141
Chapter 9 ~ Passage Through Narrow Spaces	169
Chapter 10 ~ Twists and Turns of Being in Athens	211
Chapter 11 ~ Resolutions Between Worlds	239
Post Script ~ 1	255
Post Script ~ 2	259
About The Author	263
Other Books, Essays, and Poems By Ambika Talwar	265
Final Meditations	269

Introduction

All who are intent on self-knowledge know the journey as an archetype of tremendous power, how desire and shadow hide and dance in the psyche before the physical journey is conceived or planned. A single journey can be sparked by something completely out of the ordinary or something as commonplace as a conversation or seminar. Whatever it is, it must be a deep inner calling that responds to a shout from the universe.

Out of the blue in late spring 2002, I received information about a screenwriting program being offered in Greece. I decided it would be a terrific opportunity to visit a country long in my imagination. After all, who has not studied Greek mythology in school or college? Greece had been a place of fascination to me since my school days in India. Stories of gods and goddesses that I read as a teen had revealed to me their ways, some more human than divine. How they created worlds, revealed the human-divine connection, influenced psyche and shadow in narratives, which even today temper our longing for wholeness. Somehow, in the present time, I had been magically drawn towards Greek cultural events in Los Angeles.

Several months prior to this visit, I found myself with new friends in the Greek community, which led to me attending classes in *Sirtaki,* Greek dance. Some of the music to which we danced was reminiscent of old Hindi film tunes, wherein the notes too dance between spaces like grapevines along crisscrossed railings. I became curious about Greek rituals and was invited to festivals held at the local Greek Orthodox Church. Then it was natural that I chose to attend the *epitaphios* ceremony of the Greek Easter before departing for the ancient land. I can say with certainty that diverse world traditions recognize the significant power of the five elements of which we are made—earth, water, fire, air, ether—in various ceremonies. Such synchronicities were pointing the way to my impending visit to Greece. So, I chose to make it happen, and the universe elegantly cohered with my choice and intention.

I would participate in the screenwriting seminar in Greece and remain there longer with the intention of staying on an island to write a screenplay of a twisted romance in a land of butterflies. I had envisioned learning about the mating rituals of butterflies, so I could use this information as a parallel for my story of romance and adventure. Furthermore, I had wished for something out of the ordinary, a change from my teaching at the college, a reassessment of my own desires and interests, and I longed to discover new depths of understanding of my own psyche's creative potential. What better place than a land so layered in mythic structures that had influenced much of Western culture in all disciplines of learning and one that was embroiled in its own complications in the changing economic structures of Europe!

What more would be revealed to move me, I did not know. When asked what plans I had made and what I wanted to do; I said events would unfold as they are meant to. Spontaneous traveling can be difficult but also adventurous, leading one in and out of grand and playful surprises and challenges.

As I waited for the flight at the Los Angeles Airport, I began to wonder what lay ahead even as my heart felt alive dancing in a state of uncertainty. I wondered at my purpose and a voice spoke: *I want Greece to liberate me from myself.* I had no inkling what this would lead to or what events would shift my foundations. But this little seed spread a carpet before me that would take me through narrow places, high and low places to carve myriad paths, a hundred questions, and a longing to discover my hidden selves.

So began my journey through this ancient land as I longed for greater illumination. I chose to release the anxiety of travel; instead, I chose to taste the world's rich flavors, as they would arrive. I chose to surrender to the Oracle, to the gods, to the Mothers, to adventures in the buried sites and crumbling cities and to what in me was unformed.

There is something to be said for developing mindfulness, a state of awareness permitting myself to venture into new ways. I learned this state calls for greater gratitude and humility, so we may experience being empty. Some refer to this state as being mindless—less mind and more awareness.

Whispering icons whose eyes
paean of hope and despair
long to awaken, to ascend...

Come! Arrive in me, I say.
Reveal to me manifestations of renewal.

Instead, the descent—oneiros
takes me deeper into the painted
and fading faces of antiquity.

Will I get lost in forms and dust of historia?

Will I find Poseidon in posters alive as in dream?

Will I walk with Athena in stone
as she breathes life into olive trees—
gains a city and adoration?

Will I sup with Dionysus dancing in mosaic
not pixels of mini-DV... in crumbling caves
temples to deities in the dust ...?

What of Areté and Sophia?
When where did we all lose them?

Is our evolution a movement from
one technology to another?

23

the anvil of the wordsmith
the furnace, a hidden heart
rhythms of a future memory

Do we recreate the same forms
in narratives we think are new?

Like a puppet strung
in many directions, I close my eyes

Who are we?
        Where are we going?

            Why?

"Life is an unfoldment, and the further we travel the more truth we can comprehend. To understand the things that are at our door is the best preparation for understanding those that lie beyond."

~ Hypatia

Chapter 1 ~ Arrivals

With a deep sigh of relief and the eagerness of a child, I see we have finally landed at Athens International Airport. It is somewhere between where the 9th of June passages into the 10th in the year 2002. I follow the groggy wave of passengers to the baggage pick-up area and wait for my bags to come rolling rumbling almost gracefully down the conveyer belt. The airport is not very big and not so busy past midnight. I feel strange landing in a new place at this odd time.

After eight long grueling hours in Zurich—a city I decided I was not ready to be in love with—and another near three sleepy hours on a plane, I hope never again to be on a plane for this long a time. Already in another time zone both mentally and physically, I feel sort of "spaced out." This spacey-ness lends a surreal quality that makes everything take on a different life, with images within images with or without auras, floating in and out of portals. It is what I am doing here—floating in and out of portals...and auras.

Landing at the airport, I sense a shadow of discouragement, maybe even disappointment for the Greeks have lost their ancient drachma to the currency in vogue. I have neither *drachmas* nor Euros so I am unable to rent a cart. The airport feels deserted; I will learn soon how the transition to the Euro has affected Greece. A hint of scarcity adds to my feeling of discombobulation and inability to take right action. Or so I think. An elderly man offers me space in his cart for my bags. I decline and say I am waiting for someone. But he insists I place my suitcase in his cart. He comes out with me. I am a bit nervous at this assistance from a stranger; I do not want to be misunderstood. We step out and the night sky with stars greets us. This lifts my spirit.

27

Thankfully, I see Athanas Petrou waiting by his car down the road. He pulls up by me, lifts my suitcase from the cart and puts it in his car. I thank the older man who then departs.

Athanas is a portly balding man with a rotund build. We had met in Los Angeles where he had come to teach about bio-energy medicine. Interested in the diverse field of holistic medicine, I had spent some time learning about his work at a seminar. He had insisted that were I ever to come to Greece, I should stay with him and his wife. Here he is waiting to take me to the home he shares with his wife and children, with his mother and mother-in-law, and employees who work in his home-office.

Thaleia, Athanas' charming wife, stands framed by the door when we arrive in the car rumbling down a small sloping cobbled lane off a main road I learn is called Metamorfoseos. I smile a wee smile as I recall how synchronous is this name with my journey.

I pull my bags out of the boot, then Athanas drives away to park. The small narrow street is packed with dinky cars. I enter the house and become acquainted with Thaleia, about whom I have known almost nothing. Nor have I seen pictures. Athanas had simply said to me back in Los Angeles that the way to see her is to visit.

Once inside, I find that I am surrounded by furniture, idols, and curios; their home looks like a crowded museum of kitsch in chaos. Movement seems difficult in this room where curios run against each other in a strange happenstance—I am used to more open spaces. But this will be my base in Greece, and I must become used to it, learn to take all in stride. I know I won't fall over things or break them. At least, I hope not.

The perfect hostess, Thaleia, warm-hearted, short and wide of girth and with beautiful red hair, smilingly makes us some tea and we sit in the backyard chatting. She speaks a broken English, but we manage. Then Athanas carries my bags up the stairs to a room on the terrace. This will be my room for some weeks; I like that it is up on the terrace. It is a feat for him to take the suitcases up the narrow winding wrought iron stairs that meet regular cement stairs midway. I am reminded of the symbolism of the phrase "the narrow place" meaning a passage for tuning in to a kind of poetry; the narrow place, passage of difficulty, of suffering before the mystical illumination.

Thaleia tells me her mother, unwell for many months, is in a room downstairs. Sensing great unease in Thaleia naturally tense over her mother's illness, I listen. She speaks in Greek, and I wonder what I can say. I do not know yet just how sick is the dying lady, Galatea.

Athanas returns to show me upstairs. It is now three early hours into Monday, June 10. I climb the stairs with him and realize the difficulty he has in taking the bags to the room on the terrace. The staircase winds steeply, posing a challenge for a man with a cardiac problem. But stepping out into this open space brings calm. It is nice here. He has arranged lights along the walls and also installed what is a very large pagoda-like structure.

I like looking at rooftops of homes in the neighborhood. Here I see a jagged symphony of rooftops, mostly old buildings, some with plants, some broken like chipped teeth, but all homely and well used edging their way into the sky. They remind me strangely of parts of New Delhi or Calcutta—old with peeling walls, damp with sweat of time and monsoon. They remind me of possibilities strung out, stretching and somehow lingering, stuck or sticking for a while, as moss and mold take their hold in crevices—stories forgotten and hard to pull out into the light. Terraces are often romantic spaces, where people meet for cocktails, for clandestine kisses, or to store broken boxes and plants in pots that need watering.

In the old days, people used their terraces for parties, for summer sleep outs under the stars, for hideaway romancing. Now, with work pressures, people seem to remain in their homes in the evenings, too tired to climb to the top, too preoccupied with life's foibles and dilemmas to enjoy that quiet relaxing drink on the terrace with the evening breeze. That was part of another time and culture. Now the maid may come up and hang clothes to dry on the terrace. Calcutta rooftops in Athens—old cities, both wet and hot. Then there are terraces for opulent parties. While some well-designed homes may have terraces for private and communal gatherings, California apartments lack this added space as building codes are concerned about safety. Too many rules curb romance...mayhem rises in dark alleys; roof-tops are for daredevil antics.

Before I bid my host good night and settle in; he tells me that if I hear a woman screaming in the morning to not be alarmed—it is his mother and since she does not know me, she might during her careless meandering wonder why there is a stranger in the house and make wild noises. Okay, I say, wondering about the layers of myth and voices that old walls reveal. I don't know that she lives on the second floor, just below the terrace. Her rooms are on the same level as the room converted into an office, which Athanas uses for his work and where his employees make sure his papers are in order.

I shut the door, fall wearily into my bed of blue sheets, turn over and close my eyes. It feels wonderful to stretch out in a real bed, to allow the 8-hour Zurich experience to seep out of my bones.

At close to 11 a.m., I am awakened by a phone call. Athanas calls to wish me good morning and to say he is leaving in thirty minutes. I pull myself out of bed, put on a wrap, wash my face, drink some water to feed my parched senses, and step downstairs ever so cautiously. Thaleia, the wife with beautiful red hair, has left for work; Athanas, the big boss, is in his office. Here I meet Tzimis and Meropi, both employees at Athanas' company, which has a manufacturing plant not far from the house. I remember that I had spoken to Meropi on the phone some weeks earlier. Tzimis' job is to research for Athanas, and Meropi, an Albanian with sweet gentle features, handles other office chores, like the phone and correspondence. She is particularly helpful in answering my queries about public transport in the city and promises to accompany me one day.

I borrow, from no one actually, a book on vortices from a table downstairs and take it upstairs with me. The tea I make feels invigorating; I read the book for about an hour and go back to sleep, a sleep that becomes stranger as it stretches into new territory. I travel into the dying woman's head. Having just arrived, I have not seen her nor been into the room, but I see into her brain. I feel as though I am traveling in a vortex and making a connection. There is a shadow on both sides of her pineal gland. One shadow presses against the other shadow, squeezing the pineal gland further into darkness—it is the one gland that thrives on light, the absence of which is a major cause of depression, which is brought on by various other causes or triggers. I wonder if this shadow is a growth of some kind; it has a malevolent presence. It does not represent life energy, but a shutting down—*kaput*, the end. Swimming between vortices into a deep sinking slumber, I awake late in the afternoon, sometime close to 2 p.m.

One more cup of tea, then I bathe and go downstairs at 3 p.m. I find myself in the living room and sit with a book in one of the comfortable sofas. At a little after 3, the front door opens and Thaleia enters. We greet one another; she is apologetic but rushed as she is summoned inside to her mother's room. Everything happens very fast. She hurries out calling in a loud and pained voice to her husband who dashes out of their bedroom and together they go in to see her mother, Galatea. I am on the couch, freshly bathed and jet-lagged, feeling helpless, a little embarrassed and much concerned.

Sometimes, there's nothing one can do and final attempts at revival are but futile. Athanas later tells me that early morning at 4, they had revived her, but this time it didn't work. Three stories above in my room, where I lay passed out with jet lag, I had neither heard nor witnessed anything. Paris, their older boy, had also tried mouth to mouth—it didn't work. Bion, the younger son, had sat nervous and praying by her side. They pumped her chest—it didn't work.

All the while, I stand outside wondering if there's anything I can do; I know there isn't. I also don't want to intrude in the family space. I have just arrived. We don't know one another. I know the husband only from a class he had taught in the USA on energy medicine. He is a scientist who

31

has developed a machine that delivers a form of energy medicine, one that works with frequencies to monitor and to return one to a state of balance.

Then in a trice there is commotion. Thaleia comes out of her mother's room and makes a flurry of phone calls. In what feels like a few seconds, people show up. I bring Thaleia a glass of water, but she cannot take any. I recall I have somehow the charge to bring water to people in trying circumstances—I'd brought water to my grandmother when *Beji*, her mother, had died and we were at a gathering to remember her. Water—an element of life. Revival. I feel helpless without it. I feel helpless unless I can offer water. Now, I am learning to be still—sometimes, that is what people need, or maybe I do.

First arrives Milos, Athanas' cousin's son; a short heavyset young man, he works as a clerk in Athanas' small-scale factory. Then Thaleia's aunt and uncle, then Selene, Milos' mother, and more and more people. I, an outsider, stand somewhere curiously watching the tragic drama unfold that brings the community huddling into this crowded space. A dark-eyed woman in somber but fancy shades of beige comes from a funeral service, sobs with Thaleia *"Po po po po..."* commiserates for an hour or so and leaves. More relatives and friends arrive. Damali, about eleven or twelve, clings to Thaleia when the mourner hits intense notes. I learn that this moaning is a tradition practiced to make people mourn. I learn that it is also the same cry one makes in joyful circumstances to congratulate. *"Po...po...po...po...!"*

Athanas suggests I sit outside in the backyard. He sits with me. We are met with Tzimis and Meropi and some other people from the laboratory down the street. Damali comes to sit with Athanas, who introduces his daughter to me. She is a quiet one, unlike other family members.

Half of the backyard of Athanas' and Thaleia's home is lined with marble and decorated with plants; the other half is plain dirt with small trees and a clothesline or two where they dry their laundry. This is like back home, where Ma also hangs clothes out to dry, not in the monsoons. Except here when they are in a hurry, they use the electric dryer built into the

32

washer. White cottons dry well in the sun, but colored clothes fade.

In all this commotion, Thaleia even manages to apologize for not taking care of me. Oh dear, I say-think-feel, "Thaleia, it is I who am so sorry. Please, do not worry about me." Is there anything I can do? Not really, except to stay out of the way and if anything is needed, then to offer my services.

In the meanwhile, more people arrive. Selene remains busy in the kitchen. She and Daiya (the Polish woman who works for the Petrou family) prepare food. I sit with Tzimis and Meropi in the yard and listen to conversations when the food arrives. We eat together fish-vegetable stew and Greek salad greens peppered with *feta,* black olives, sprinkled with lemon and olive oil.

The afternoon is filled with visitations of friends paying condolence. Endings and beginnings mark our lives, sometimes quietly and sometimes in the midst of commotion.

Melpo & Galatea

An old woman, with a clear radiant complexion, light eyes, silver hair, comes into the kitchen and is led outside to the yard. Athanas calls me and introduces me to his mother. I look at her intently as she is the one he had warned me about—the woman wailing in the dark on cloudless nights, sometimes moonstruck. I am curious and wonderstruck. Can she be mad? I want to forget that he has told me of her craziness.

I look into the eyes of one of the most beautiful women I have ever seen: "Grandmother Melpomene," as he calls her. She's 97 and her eyes sparkle with a mischief and, paradoxically, also with serenity. Her sweetness resides in her bones in a self-contented way as she speaks to me, repeating from moment to moment her question: "You like Greece?" Taken in by her lovely eyes, I do not know yet how mad she can be. Perhaps she's just mildly unbalanced as I soon learn she is given to expressing a mean and nasty temper, screaming at people and hitting at things when she loses

33

control. Moreover, she cannot remember anything from one minute to the next. So they tell me. She is the one who goes screaming down hallways and stairs when she has lost the mask of composure. Her hair shines silvery white at all times of the day and night.

Selene, a kind unassuming woman, is still busy in the kitchen, making coffee for guests. She makes me some too, "no sugar, no milk" at my request. When I finish the coffee, I pour the remains on the saucer. Then Mama Melpo, the silver-haired grandmother, reads the coffee grounds in my mug. "You have a long journey ahead of you," she says, "a very long journey." She looks at me and wishes me *"Kalo droma"* a number of times. Then she looks again at the coffee grains and says I'll marry a rich man and she smiles. Her eyes sparkle wildly, playfully; sometimes, they glower with a sharp focus. Okay, I say, wondering if this isn't what every reader tells every single woman—that everything will end happily ever after. But I am open to the greatest of possibilities from the universe whose stories keep us going. Sometimes we survive by stories; sometimes we get lost in them.

Grandmother "Kyria" Melpo keeps holding my hands, kisses me from time to time. Tzimis, the researcher, laughs and says she is strong and will outlive everyone. She will never die, he says. And her eyes, he says, were made better and stronger with special bio-energy treatments; he is, of course, speaking of the system he uses that was developed by Athanas. Tzimis continues with, "She is so tough that she climbs over the wall into the neighbor's yard—that is when and how she forgets where her own home is." All this time Kyria Melpo sits in her serene manner outside with me and with relatives. She keeps looking at me with twinkling eyes. She likes what she sees but notes I am too thin. Delicate shades of my grandmother, Mimi, in an old familiar landscape whispering: "You girls are too thin...you should eat more."

Athanas comes out and asks me to bid farewell to the friends and relatives. Meropi and I go in. The body is already in the coffin—the hearse has arrived. Some men carry the coffin outside to the car; somebody breaks a plate; the van leaves. The women in unison wail, *"Po...po...po..."* They are in black. The children are encouraged to also moan but to step back away from the coffin. Damali watches curious and sad in her faded dress.

We return to the yard. Athanas tells me that Galatea, Thaleia's mother, had been ailing for some time. When Thaleia returned home from work earlier in the day and went in to see Galatea, she had not been in for more than a few seconds, when Galatea said, *"Parakalo,"* and left this world. *"Parakalo"* is a way of saying "please," but it has various shades of meaning: sometimes it is said as a way to deflect praise, sometimes a way to say "let me help." In this case, I wonder what Galatea meant, or to whom she addressed this final word.

Parakalo
Open the door
I am ready

Athanas tells a lingering relative who wants to know more that they had been up at 4:00 a.m. and he had at that time brought her back, but not this time some hours later. "I maintained her for six months. Something had been wrong with her brain...the doctors had not been able to tell us what," he says. She had been leaving this world very slowly. In the morning when Thaleia left for work, she had told her mother to wait for her to get back home. Galatea had done so. Now I see what had been bothering Thaleia the night before. This time of separation was drawing near, and they had all been caught in the warp of uncertainty.

Hours after Galatea died, Athanas, who is scheduled to give a lecture on Steven Hawking, is ready to go. The boys are told they must stay home with their mother and sister. Tzimis, Meropi and I accompany him. After that, at Athanas' request, I drive Tzimis to pick up some furniture. In Athens for less than twenty-four hours and I am already driving their old car! I am pleased that I very easily get into the flow of traffic despite jet lag. Roads are being worked on for the Olympics in 2004.

35

Tzimis seems very comfortable with my driving and says, "Is like you were always driving here." Quite comfortable in the driver's seat, I keep my hands on the wheel and my fingers crossed; I feel like a heroine. It is imperative that one drive in Los Angeles; I had driven very little in India, where traffic is erratic as it is here, but here it is less dense. Sometimes, jet lag makes one give up worrying; one just does what one must.

Then Tzimis starts to speak about human energy systems and time travel, about past life regressions, about seeing visions, about psychic phenomena. At first I hesitate, then I tell him that just before I'd gone back to sleep around noon earlier that day, I'd seen what might have been wrong with Galatea. My mind had swirled into visions and I had sunk into a deep stupor, a strange sleep no doubt made intense by jet lag, but I'd gone into another dimension into spaces that are private, and, therefore, sacred, into Galatea's consciousness, into her brain space—and beyond it. I was more than ever convinced that I had journeyed deep into her space and wondered why I was chosen to be the seer.

I'd seen a dark shadow on both sides of her pineal gland. Perhaps, there was a tumor on one side that created pressure on the other side. I ask him questions about her. He tells me that she lived in darkness most of her life—her rooms were perpetually dark as though it were always night. After her husband died ten or so years ago, she had shut down all the windows of the house. She had them covered with black paper. She had drenched herself with darkness.

Now it is confirmed. This knowing was part of my journey of expanding my awareness.

I think of uncertainties, events that are never planned, how a single moment can change the direction of a journey.

I will recall the image of women along many village streets, aging in black dresses, already cowled unto death. It will sadden me—I will recall the widows of Brindaban, an ancient Indian city, where Lord Krishna, the blue-skinned flute-playing god, is said to have been born. A city of legend and temples, Brindaban now has charities that provide shelter at a big price. Hindu widows in empty rooms chant until their last days and are kept alive by trusts, which are often false promises in a corrupt system. That image, too, had twisted my heart.

Long graying years are chanted away without family, without end. What vows held them in perpetual seclusion *sans joie* or companionship, no matter what their age, young and old alike and some even left there as girl brides become girl widows, whose state included sexual exploitation— karmic woes chained to cultural conditions made oppressive by patriarchal traditions.

But aren't karmic laws simply beliefs used to manage people? It cannot all be tit-for-tat. Karma is about actions one takes in response to another action. If it were solely payback, no one would ever get out of this oppressive cycle. We are also triggered and move by choice.

Here in Athens, I learn Galatea had chosen darkness and had refused any and all holistic treatments, even the work developed by Athanas. The pineal gland needs light in order to function to its optimum and to illumine spiritual light. But Galatea lived in darkness; the pineal gland remained unfed for the last ten years of her life—as long as she'd been a widow. Had the light gone out of her life when her husband died? Perhaps, she had always lived in the dark. To whom do women make the vow to remain joyless and why?

I shared this insight with Athanas who wondered how I could have seen this as I hadn't ever met her and only seen her body after her death. "No, I don't have to see her," I'd replied. We are part of the cosmic weave and may be invited by another consciousness to interact. For some reason, she allowed me to see this. Or maybe it was God. Not everything one sees or knows exists on the material plane. But this journey into Galatea's brain left its mark on my mind. I still recall a strange heaviness of traveling into a person's space, someone whom I had not met or known.

Who knows what thoughts and images that one experiences or is privy to that are not even one's own! We often think other people's thoughts and claim them as ours. We must be aware of this.

Somehow, I was meant to be a part of her last rites. I remember my old dream of three to four years ago, in which I had seen a special blue light on the eighth floor of a building where I am assigned to help people pass into the other world. I also recall my last moments with Paddy, a friend's husband, how I had held his head gently in my hands—perhaps this speeded his process and allowed him to release old patterns and disturbing memories. I remember his last hours although I wasn't with him—I felt it all in my body and I felt ill. At a concert, I couldn't feel at ease, but was unsettled, anxious and in pain. A friend who had taken me to the concert brought me back home. As soon as we reached home from the concert, there was a call from Carrie, Paddy's wife. She told me he'd died at about the time that I'd been feeling ill. I had felt and known the end when it came. This was two years ago.

Fate and human consciousness work in strange ways, mysteriously intertwined. What may seem like chance could be human action; what may seem like human motivation might well be fate. So it is with journeys planned or unplanned.

I mused to myself that after I had completed my packing in Los Angeles I'd thrown in a black dress at the last minute. I had wondered why I'd want to wear black in the intolerably hot temperatures of Greek summer. I smile with irony at the twists that bring us into deeper connections. Such happenings make us part of each other—I become part of the family.

Sometimes, a journey begins with a funeral.

wind trembling leaf spirals in vast space
I disappearing ... spanda
reveals unities

"The gods, likening themselves to all kinds of strangers, go in various disguises from city to city, observing the wrongdoing and the righteousness of men."

~ Homer

Chapter 2 ~ Departures

It is Tuesday, 11th of June. Athanas, Thaleia, and I leave for Lefkada to attend the funeral. It is a six-hour drive. Kyrie Melpo had said I could look forward to a long journey. It is only now beginning. I doze off and on while our charioteer Athanas drives us to Lefkada. At Patra we take a boat to the island, disembark at Rio Anterio and continue the drive. At Nidra we meet with their longtime friends whose car has broken down. They go with us to the service, which is supposed to start at 5 but starts at 4 p.m. We barely make it.

I am not sure why the time had been moved up. Maybe it was because of the heat and people were tired of waiting in its intensity.

We arrive at a small Orthodox church with barely enough space for thirty to sit; now there are probably over sixty people standing in a tight crowd. The heat heightens everything. The room smells intensely bucolic with garlic, heat, fatigue, unwashed clothes, and sweaty tears. The coffin is displayed in the center of the room. Thaleia enters and falls weakly onto her knees with grief. Her mother has gone, never to return, and here is the body dressed and decorated with flowers. Selene and the Polish Daiya hold up Thaleia with the strength they can together muster and bring her out; then we drive to the house. We change into clean black clothes and return to the church.

The service is short. People greet the relatives after walking around the coffin in which Galatea's body would lie for the next three years after which they will remove her bones and put them in an urn, says Selene. Both down to earth and a romantic at the same time, Selene is practical in dealing with matters and knows how to laugh and to dream.

Once the service is over, Galatea's body is taken to the cemetery beside the church. No loitering or lingering. The coffin is lowered, the dirt thrown over the coffin—the final act is done. Bottles of *Metaxa* sit on a table with some plastic cups near the wall of the cemetery, but we leave for the house. I have taken some pictures, but not without asking the quiet and gentle Selene for permission. She says it is okay.

At the house, Selene and other women are busy laying out a variety of biscuits, pouring cups of *metaxa* and making Greek coffee, *kafé nero*. Selene makes some without sugar for me, for the priest, and for herself.

I notice that the dress of the women of Lefkada includes a layered bodice, which they wear with a scarf that covers the bosom, which is not covered by the dress but by a layer under the dress. I wonder at the logic of leaving the breasts uncovered and then dropping a scarf over it. I wonder if it served a function of nursing babies. Thaleia's aunt has a dress similar to this one; she says I can wear hers back in Athens.

We stay the night in Lefkada. Friends of the family, including Angela and her husband, Selene, Athanas and I sit at Petros' Kafé. Petros is a likeable sort—a bit of a rake, playful, wild. Petros supplies us with a variety of fish preparations. Small fish soaked in vinegar, which Angela tells me is raw, does not taste so bad. The other smaller fish fried whole tastes really good, but I forget the name of this silvery being.

After partaking of fish, jokes, and stories, I leave for a short walk and return to the house. Drink some coffee and eat some biscuits. Jet lag insists on permeating my being, making this whole experience surreal. Forgotten are the beaches of Los Angeles; here is a Greek island, a funeral, and lots of people I will never see again. It feels like a moment from the Odyssey, a descent into another time and space, meeting with characters unique, independent, bizarre, and curious.

Time tastes different in different lands. I am an observer, participating in a familial ritual. I see more women in black. More *kafé nero*. More brandy. More cookies. I am also the observed. We all observe one another. We are curious.

I ask if I may take pictures, particularly of Efthalia, a seventy-year-old woman who lives alone and is friend of Galatea. She's tiny and dressed in black from head to toe. I remember her beside Galatea's lifeless body in the church. She'd stood by the head, warding off flies, her way of caring for her dead friend. Then she'd followed others as they walked round the body before meeting relatives and then had returned to her place by Galatea. There in the sweltering heat and crowded room while her eyes expressed a connection with the proceedings, she remained touchingly self-contained: her petite build, her sweet concern, her final gestures for an old friend—the warding off of flies.

Here she is in front of me—Efthalia, smilingly and with probing eyes asking who I am—I am a stranger to these parts. Athanas tells her I have come from Los Angeles. I wonder what roads of destiny insisted on bringing me to this place on my second day in Greece. Back in my ancient land, they say that on every single grain of food is written its eater's name—*daane daane par likha hai khaane waale ka naam*. Such an idiom must have risen from stories in rural parts where wandering guests were invited to partake of meals as they passage through strange villages on their way. It speaks of hospitality and generosity of people of the soil.

We stay the night in Lefkada and wake early to leave for Athens, where Athanas is to teach a class at around noon. In the car, I ask him why all the women we've seen while driving were dressed in black. I understand that black is for mourning, but were all the villages in mourning? He said they wear black when someone dies. Custom dictates they stay in black for three years; by then someone else dies, and then someone else, and so on. This sounds grim to me. He laughs; I wonder. Is everyone always in mourning? Is this how women live the second half of their lives?

The drive is long and I feel drowsy. Hunger pangs make chaos in my belly, but I find nothing on the way that I can eat. Athanas stops somewhere along the way at a small wayside *kafé* and eats a huge chunk of apple pie—sugary and tasty no doubt, but I decline. A big bulky pastry in this heat does not invite. We drive on; I fall into deep slumber, the heat

43

seeping into my bones as the sun aslant pours its warmth generously, mercilessly without regard.

> *Buried near stones*
> *a body seeks dissolution*
> *Heat severs desires*

> *a soul's longing*
> *wings away into forever skies...*

> *Will she turn around*
> *to see what remains..?*

Reaching Athens

We finally reach Athens, the great city that is to host the Summer Olympics in 2004. To prepare for this momentous event, the city is being primed with repairs of old roads and buildings. Many streets are broken for re-construction. Piles of rubble and other materials create heavy congestion leading to drivers' frustration exacerbated by the heat. I get an eyeful of this ancient city being given a facelift in the midst of a financial crisis about to worsen. Greece's surrendering her drachma for the euro has made bread very costly. The financial burden weighs heavily on the common man, whose numbers are growing.

Once in the city, Athanas shares his concerns regarding his beloved Athens—he decries the work of city planners that has created traffic jams. "All the streets have become one-way," he complains. He believes this is part of the plan to slow down people and prevent progress, stunt growth and creativity of all kinds. Environment affects a people's growth. In this ever-increasing corporate landscape of grey cement and piles of concrete and roadblocks, people easily lose sense of identity and direction. Such a loss seems to be pervasive in many communities worldwide.

Once we reach home, I feel utterly ravenous. Rowena, a young and lovely maid, fixes me some lunch after which I go to sleep. A very deep and heavy sleep suffuses my eyes, my hair, my arms, my all. I sleep despite the noise of people building a roof over newly built corridors of this house. I awake two hours later, get ready and go downstairs. Of course, it is always time for tea.

Athanas has suggested I go to the Akropolis. It turns out that Meropi can go with me. That is nice. We share a birthday. It's good to have company. We take the metro to the Akropolis, walk around there for some time, then go on down to the Plaka, sit at a *kafé* with a snack.

Here, Konstantine, a tall, gaunt, fifty-ish man, who works at the *kafé* tells me that we are related—he and I. Because he's Greek and I am Indian, and that philosophically we are close, and that it's all mathematics anyway. He remarks that my coming here at this time seems right. I must smile at his comment. Perhaps in the cosmic scheme of things, it is mathematically accurate, correct. It's an affirmation of a point in any journey, a process of perhaps understanding or illumining the purpose of a journey and of a longing for some type of completion or opening—I do not know the numbers. However, even though we have free will, I see that our destiny is influenced by movement in the skies.

Is each one of us a necessary part counted in the vast infinite cosmos? Do we matter? Perhaps, if we learned to revere our environs, we would be better influencers.

Man is a thread in the weave, an intimate part of the rhythmic arrangement of heavenly bodies, the planets, stars, asteroids, and meteors. In seeing ourselves as part of this intricate cosmic design and computing it mathematically through astronomy and, perhaps even astrology, we can understand ourselves and our myriad relationships. Look at coordinates of transformation and change in the skies; naturally, we are affected by it all.

But is each of us necessary to the unfolding cosmic destiny? Do we truly matter? Ought we not to be better influencers? Learn to revere our environs?

I wonder if it is this he is suggesting, that we are all connected. Or something more esoteric. I like the poetry of it. I muse at his stories as he serves me my order of Greek salad.

45

Yes, we are all related, I nod looking at his gaunt features textured by a deep olive complexion that must sheath his whole being.

It is all very interesting. I think I am here because I want Greece to liberate me, perhaps from myself. It is not uncommon for people to visit India for this reason, driven east by the stresses of western materialism. Deep down, of course, I realize that the answers lie within me; I must then be looking for an excavation—how to bring answers into the light, so be more self-aware.

The tall Konstantine keeps looking at me; he wants me to come back so we can talk. I nod; maybe after my trip to Kea and Thessaloniki.

I am to leave that night for Kea with a writing group arriving from the US. We must stay on schedule to travel and learn the art of good screenwriting. As it so happens in epic journeys, events can take us away from one trend to experience something else. Are these interventions caused by the all-powerful heavenly bodies whose dance across the skies is the measure of the universe, of its harmonics at the same time?

How does Fate seek
her own path
in the melding dances
of starlight?

What cosmic worm
does she swallow?

What cosmic loom
does she weave
when night's sentry
passes by?

"What I like to drink most is wine that belongs to others."

~ Diogenes

Chapter 3 ~ In Search of Stories

Of film, fruit, & frolic
sing to me ... which one
tastes more divine?

The screenwriters and scholars of the Prometheusa Writing Center based in Northern California have arrived at the Athens airport. Athanas brings me to the airport. From somewhere in the crowd of travelers, a man of medium height with gray-blonde hair and wizened face smiles and walks towards us. So I meet Seamus, facilitator of the writing group. After a quick introduction, Athanas is assured that I am in good hands. He leaves.

As Seamus shares with me details of the first leg of the journey, his wife and child and writing cohorts gather by us. From here we journey together for what is a screenwriting course, but as we will find out, it will change direction. There are about eighteen eager writers. Somehow, suddenly things happen very fast. So the next point of the journey begins with a drive to nearby Lavrio for a night's rest. For a few hours, many of us walk around at night unable to settle in. But soon we must rest for we have an early departure across a wild expanse of water.

We are ready at 6 a.m. to take the ferry to Kea, a small picturesque island. The sea is shades of deep blue—it's how the navy gets its colors. These deep blue layers of waves and the universe are in harmony—a system of associations makes sense in chaos. What overtly appears as terrifying beauty hides beneath layers of currents to reveal its horrors, for if the Fates decreed, one could meet with pernicious death glorified only if one were to rise up as a hero and save everyone from doom. Or if one were the carrier of the treasured chalice returned to save humankind from itself.

I have a lovely room in Hotel Karthea in Korissia. The door opens to a balcony, which overlooks white houses intertwined with mainly blue and some with red accents. The sky is special shades of blue, almost cerulean with a touch of lapis. The breeze is sweet and full. It blows over the hill beside which the hotel nestles.

Soon we gather for dinner and then reconvene for a scheduled discussion on screenwriting process and principles. But as we know from the epic tradition, an unplanned shift may take the event in another direction. So on our first night, we watch *Never on Sunday* (1960), a film by American director Jules Dassin who had chosen to make Greece his home. Yes, we discuss how the story unfolds in this award-winning film and review the unities of narrative structure. But our attention stays on learning of Greek culture, the love of dance and of ouzo.

The film is fabulous. The lead character, Ilya, played by one-time Greek Culture Minister Melina Mercouri and then-wife of Dassin, is wildly passionate, perfectly self-assured, and loves the good life; most of all, she loves with a grace and wit that make her a lovely humanitarian at the same time. She cannot be "civilized" by Homer, an American transplant who wants to teach her to love one person and to become proficient in the classics. He wants her to know Greek literary culture as he knows it, for, according to him, the only way to be truly accomplished in the world is to have knowledge of classical texts. The two characters reveal a Dionysian and Apollonian schism, which makes for more than lively banter. And Homer, ironically named after the great national poet, suggests the stereotype of an American intervening in another's ways so reminiscent of cultural and political domination in the last century, which sadly continues today

Homer's two-week experiment with Ilya, "a hooker with a heart of gold," is successful for a very short time, until she discovers his liaison with No-Face, the landlord who has been exploiting his tenants. This is an ironic twist on the man of morals who shows his lack of them. She returns to her former life, and the boys are overjoyed, as is the Italian who has become her "main man."

Dassin, naturally, plays with Greek mythology in his film. Medea, Melina's character insists, never killed her children. "Look, they got up and walked away after the play," she notes, bold and nonchalant.

Dassin displays an intense fascination for the story of Medea in *A Dream of Passion* (1978), a film that explores the layered Medea myth with remarkable skill and insight. It is not hard to understand why this story continues to mystify many, as it does me. Medea is a powerful idea as complex and unfathomable as the many-layered ocean that births the fire and us. A chemist and herbalist, a strong woman and mother, her action of killing her children is outrageous—as is her husband's betrayal of the marriage vows so precious to the sanctity of the bed and the emotions that bond two souls in marriage.

Truth, as we well know, is stranger than all fiction, and fiction might well illumine humanity's darkest truths. Might it be that both are same? In *A Dream of Passion*, Dassin skillfully plays with the story of a modern-day Medea. Interestingly, a small news item in *The Times of India* several years ago in New Delhi had caught my attention. I was beginning my college days; myths and motifs were fresh in my mind. The news reported the story of an American diplomat's wife who imitated Medea's actions on Father's Day in retaliation for her husband's betrayal of the sacred bed—this one not nailed to the earth by the world's axis tree but floating in the debris of unforgiving passion betraying commitment. The passion of hatred and love that run deep below the layered surfaces of waves tells harrowing tales sometimes.

In this film, Dassin chooses Mercouri to play the role of a theater actress who will naturally play Medea, while the play in the film is directed by her betraying male lover. Twists lie within twists and therein is a classic soap opera but one that defines character and morality with intense emotion and various shades of dark. In this film, she must interview the woman played by actress Ellen Burstyn, the betrayed wife and murderer of her children, in prison to know what it is like to commit a heinous crime.

On the contrary, real passion is commitment. Our myths do instruct us well, but maybe not well enough for we have erred many a time. We err with our imperfections. We err in shadow. We err from deliberate wrongdoing, from willful wrong choices, and from deliberate ignorance. Shall we now ache to arrive at a finer intelligence in all our roles with refined human capacities in perfect impregnation and regenerative power on this our beautiful planet, Earth, named for Jord, Norse goddess and mother of Thor. Thor as sky god is also rain and thunder, which keeps earth fecund, both he and Jord together participating in the cycle of renewal and propagation. Could this unity also suggest the need for a refining moral foundation in the lives of all our people?

I am pulled in many directions; life and nature are rich in their diverse offerings, in their interconnections. My musings bring me back to Dassin, who I find is fascinated by the profound experience of womanhood. In *Never on Sunday*, Dassin creates a segment portraying the women of Piraeus in revolt against the horrendous rents they must pay No Face, an extortionist. Like the women in Aristophanes' *Lysistrata* who succeed in bringing an end to war, these women succeed in having the rents lowered. Take back the power, I say.

Take Back the Night, the day too, oh do. Let's build communities where we live in joy, grace, in communion and in companionship despite differences! How may we find ourselves in a self-Self-self continuum and nullify limiting effects of our own perceptions, access the depth of our shadows of mythological meanderings over vast expanse of time? Where? When shall we wake up to what is precious and holy?

I miss a kind of profound simplicity in much of cinema that is made today in Hollywood, so woefully loyal to computer-generated images that inner dramatic intensity suffers, and the story remains distant from human passions and the play of the inner landscape, its joys and sorrows. Too much is on the surface, much that keeps us distant from each other thereby furthering the ache. Everything must happen "fast-fast"—car chases, flip dialogues so "cute-cute" or "sexy-sexy" and shooting guns and splattering blood. The Indian film scene centered in Bollywood, too, has its excesses of graphic vulgar violence and melodrama.

Bollywood layers epic stories with so much melodramatic glue that essence is lost; tear up hearts with a sharpened cleaver and there are not enough tears to wash wounds but carpets in homes lie stained with dross. How can our cultures find a way out of this mess of unholy emotions while media doyens insist, "But it is what the masses want!" Instead, people are programmed by the influence of the story makers into an addiction that keeps them from clarifying their lives.

It has been the age of the potboiler—a sad reflection of the power of moneymakers who program people and are also caught in this web of disinfotainment.

Perhaps, there will be a change in perception and a desire for a new aesthetic. Times change, as do priorities. While plot-driven stories without depth in character still emblazon the screen and most definitely television, there are some that also invite introspection. People must be hungry for it. Bollywood, too, repeats its formula in the majority of films, but when they break from it and subvert old paradigms, they birth genius, which becomes a mythic gift suggesting an evolving presence for individuals and the nation. Older films of the highly respected Satyajit Ray, Mrinal Sen, and the more recent Ketan Mehta and the aesthetically pleasing Anurag Basu remind us of genius we ache for—ours and everyone's so we can commune with wonder together.

Possibly the reason why I feel a communal distance is that this lovely city of angels is one dictated by geography and cultural boundaries, a certain ghetto-ization of neighborhoods. We all thus become busily involved in our "projects," whatever they may be. Being single in a big city can be problematic. One's life begins to revolve around oneself, one's must-do activities, and one's needs, which one can forget easily. One loses some kind of layering that comes with playing different roles in life; one gains other things—a freedom to come and go as one pleases. A freedom to "be lost"—I recall a very recent conversation with a young and upcoming opera singer. "It is easy to get lost in Los Angeles," she had noted, somewhat wistfully.

I wonder though about the other life—the one with family. I think of the one I left five thousand miles away, or did they leave me? I think of my mother who had wondered why we part and stay so far away. I'd answered, "So I can write about you." It sounds strange now that she would say such a thing. Does she forget why I moved here? And my father, whose eyes reveal ambivalence about so much, when heart and mind spar? How we are touched by longing and by lineage, which affect our destiny in mysterious ways!

There are others on this trip in the same place as I— even as we discover a commonality, I know we will not see each other again. Promises to remain in touch are as fleeting as friendships in the hi-tech urban environment to which we have become unhappily accustomed today. We live in the moment—that is all that matters. In the moment, wondering about the past and the future.

> *Friend holds two ends*
> *of a severed rope: the present*
> *is space between the two.*
> *Which strands might she tie*
> *in this continuum of passages?*

> *Arms spread wide*
> *she releases both...*
> *a little string*
> *is an angel's wing.*

Scenes in a Little Paradise

Now we are here in the Cyclades enjoying the quiet paradise that Kea offers, a very hot paradise. Sun flicks us with scorching gazes. My skin begins to burn.

The first dinner together is in a *taverna* in Hora, a village thirty minutes away. Nico, our designated driver, drives us up the hill to the village. We walk to the village center to a family-owned *taverna,* as most are; Nico's son, Ianni, is the cook. We are served a variety of dishes—salad, *tzatziki,* then meatballs and one other meat dish. I request some *xorta,* dandelion greens, but they don't have any; instead, they serve a delicious dish of green beans and potatoes. Of course, I eat too much. It's easy to do so on holidays. I look at my cohorts. Everyone is enjoying the meal, the wine, and camaraderie. They are soaking in this new environment with verve, letting go of the tensions of day-to-day life back in the big city far away across distant seas. We must leave our familiar grounds in order to find each other and even our self.

Behind us are laid out tables in an L-shape to be occupied by local parents and teachers—school term ends this very day and they celebrate together. The kids are in the center playing games that I remember we played as kids in India. Something like "Oranges and lemons, sold for a penny..." except when we sang, it sounded like "Oranj-jesus lemon..."— kids sometimes make a sigh of excitement between syllables. So it goes until two people who form a bridge capture the one who is under their bridged arms at that very moment when the rhyme ends. This one is in Greek. To my utter dismay, I discover that my audio setting on the camera is not switched on, so I lose the singing of the children—so sweetly and utterly disarming. But watching them is a delight. I know I have good images to share.

We drive back to the hotel listening to Arletta, a popular Greek singer of folksy Greek songs. I don't know their meaning but like the sounds. Old languages have a way with me. I like what they do to my consciousness—Latin, Gaelic, Italian, Amharic, German, Swahili, and more, as I recall wistfully the sound of Punjabi songs in the dark of the bus trundling through the blackly winding landscape.

All languages are beautiful. Much depends on the intonations of the speaker—and what emerges from a roughened spirit or a tender awakened heart.

55

It is Friday, June 14. A lovely breakfast of fruit, cornflakes, many cups of tea, and *yaourti,* a delicious Greek yogurt—sweet mornings such as these start the day with promise. Imagine a conversation over breakfast—an actual sit-down breakfast—dreams, the day's adventures, and nostalgia over childhood breakfasts, for in our day-to-day lives, breaking fast is reserved for a Sunday. This communing becomes almost holy. We realize that too many etcetera control our lives; we have allowed meaningless items to govern us.

A vacation is a holiday: a time to restore. So it is holy.

Today's session is about short films. What makes a short film effective of course is developing one simple idea in preferably under fifteen minutes. Best to keep it focused on images with less talk. A short student film set in Greece unfolds with powerful images. Another one about capital punishment, though constructed with evocative camera angles, turns out to be tedious, clichéd, and somewhat pretentious. I wonder at all the elements that I may be guilty of, even as I sit here and offer my comments. My short, too, has a lot of dialogue. But as Seamus says, that's okay too—look at Preston Sturges, whose talkies are highly verbose. Mine is a serious drama about the transcendent nature of art and love. It is called *Androgyne.*

The evening is spent watching Renos Haralambidis's film *No Budget Story* (1998). We are to meet him later since he is on a film shoot. His philosophy is: "If you want to make a film, pick up the camera and shoot. We indie filmmakers cannot afford to wait for funding, not if we want to make our art. Big studios won't look in unless we have a powerful agent who can sell our stories, and before that we have to sell it to the agent. So, of course, the first prerequisite is to have a 'good idea,' and preferably a story." Stories abound. There is no dearth of them.

They reside within and without us at all times. The trick is to capture them at those odd hours when they peep out at us unawares. So we must be aware at all times. Let the story write itself. Let our fingers move. Let our characters' inner selves speak. So it goes. Perhaps, so it is also with epic

56

flows, story digressing into story into yet another story, until all is an interwoven tapestry of human dilemmas, motivations, and celebrations, as in Soviet writer Mikhail Sholokhov's two-part epic novel, *The Silent Don*. Sholokhov's magnificent epic enriches with exquisite detail the forces of change in what leads to the forming of the Soviet Union following the revolution as well as the passionate love entanglements, how each character seeks and resolves his or her destiny pulled by an inner calling and also a mysterious force beyond control.

The making of *No Budget Story* also has a fine and recent history: filmmaker Renos Haralambidis invited his friends and shot the film on video. He borrowed by "silent contract," which is agreement on human terms, an old 35 mm camera from the museum, projected his video version, shot it on 35, which he said "accounts for the grainy and unintended artsy look." It works. A supporting actor, borrowed from a psychiatric ward for a ten-day shoot, won best supporting actor award in the European Oscars. What more could one want? Renos is not shy of being recognized. He happily proclaims that publicity means better chances of receiving funding at some point. We meet him in Athens towards the end of the two-week seminar. He is street smart, witty, clever and handsomer than his on-screen presence, at least in *No Budget Story*. He is in a hurry and must leave for a meeting. It's an actor's life.

Now I rewind my story back to Kea to complete the story that was unfolding on this island.

We dine at Taverna Afri; the food here is simple and sumptuous. They bring me a huge serving of fish, far more than I can consume alone. I share it with my compatriots who are eating lamb. Again the owner is Ianni. Another Ianni. He has beautiful dark eyes; they look lined with *kohl*, but they are not.

> *Collyrium eyes dart*
> *restful on shimmering sea*
> *in search of story*

Slender Ianni's eyes have a paradoxically languid look; he does not linger or wait around, but slyly slinks away with a small mysterious smile. I watch him leave and turn around to see a woman looking at me. So I meet Sofia, who as I find out later is a psychologist in Athens. She is on the island to help Ianni and his mother at Taverna Afri for the week. She tells me she has longed to go to India for many years. I suggest she might wait for two more—she says "good". Why two years, I don't know. Perhaps a feeling triggered with information of the terrorist action from neighboring lands. Perhaps an effect and influence of cosmic interactions. Mathematics!?

We commiserate over the condition of the world. We wonder when the so-called darkness that has cast its spell over our humanity will shift and transform into something harmonious, into embodied luminosity. We wait for that which Apollo represents—balance, beauty, and joy in harmony; for that which Lord Rama can bring us—care and concern over the body politic—the land and all her people as we learn in the *Ramayana*. The seemingly longest epic ever written tells the story of Rama's journey in search of his divine beloved, Sita, who was kidnapped and held in what is now Sri Lanka. We await the loving that Kama, Agape, and Eros can awake—love and divine sexuality; for that which Draupadi, wife of the Pandavas in the *Mahabharat*, and Shabari, a poor woman who tastes every single berry and saves sweet ones for Rama, can bring us—devotion; for that which Savitri, a luminous being, reminds us of—virtues that guide our choices; for that which Sita brings—noble surrender to her integrity to herself; for that which human potential is capable of—victory over the forces of evil that have kept in check our evolutionary process; acceptance of the truth that remains hidden because we are so deceived by the makers of information, and our own filters for wanting to believe something that may not be right or true.

Alas, we are well practiced in the art of self-deception. Do we need Athena to pull the fog over and away from our eyes at her will? Or another god or more self-made gurus? Why do we choose to live with falsehood?

We call on Adi Shakti, Supreme Mother, to shake up the world, clear the shadowed doors of perception, and bring us to circles of fierce compassion.

Uncovering Layers

It must be June 15; so much has happened already. Today we are scheduled to trek down the mountainside about two and a half miles to the beaches that receive the waters in Karthea. Before driving to Karthea, we stop at a small museum in Hora. An enlightening experience unfolds in the local museum where we see the beauty of Doric, Ionic, and Corinthian columns—the power of grace and geometry to create lines of elegance marking hallways with stature. It is thrilling to discover that powerful Athena has also appeared as goddess with serpents—perhaps, a result of syncretism. Most likely we know that Shakti, embodied Goddess loosely vital force, energy, akin to electricity or "*vidyut*" ("u" not as in "but" but a brief short "you") all over the world has been associated with serpent, bull, lion, tiger, deer, elephant, peacock and other birds and animals.

The serpent goddess of Crete is reborn from the head of Zeus as the goddess of wisdom for the new age that followed. But before then Goddess held a deep primordial place in the culture; it was She who commanded the movement of the cosmos and mysteries. Minoan figurines with serpents in their hands tell us of the power of fertility goddesses. We find such representations appear in Egypt, Cypress, Palestine, African nations, and other lands, the serpent being associated with fertility, renewal, and transformation. In the Indian system, serpent power stands also for fearlessness, union of earth and sky as often deities have a serpent around their neck and shoulder.

The more we delve into our early histories, the more we discover deep connections with ancient cultures. Gods and goddesses reappear in different forms and with names suggestive of local lore, tenets, the wily subconscious, and the grand collective.

59

Far in the Indic plains, Ganga is born from head of Shiva. She waters the plains and mountains, making them fertile. In another age, when the world was destroyed by water, Shiva contained the excesses; when mankind roiled in drought, he released the power of his daughter, Ganga, to feed Earth to make her fecund again.

As Mother Kali is all-Cosmic process, She is cosmic Time, eternal and stupendous, magnificent and infinite, was always and is in the eternally arriving now. We remember! We long. Mother Kali is our beloved for her fierce tenderness, supreme loving, and dissolution of what must cease.

But is this cyclic process of dying into new creation evolutionary?

We remember that matri-focal systems all over the world were replaced by patriarchal systems in which male gods adopted female goddesses of the old cultures, ones that, it is posited, were developed with nurture and endurance. But the new systems changed all this and co-opted female deities making them consorts, or daughters, of the new male gods. So patriarchal systems took over, thrived, and enforced their principles thereby becoming masters of newly conquered ancient lands that appropriated existing systems of grammar, which may have lost a sacredness, as suggested in some early symbols. Then conquering became a way of life, a way to rule by domination. It is tragic that our history is lacking in narratives that speak of a more harmonious way to be, so we maintain a dominator patriarchal worldview as true. Alas, we have been too long caught in aggressive shadows that have not been resolved.

Sadly, this trend has continued in our times, leaving the fate of our humanity in ruthless hands—but a new awareness is emerging and people are seeking alternative ways to live and relate. The dread of vile militancy rises, and it must be expunged from our cellular memory and consciousness. How can such a change be inspired? Is it too late? Where languishes our self-willed awareness?

Many of us who live in conflict and uncertainty at the same time ache to revere, re-learn, create and practice harmonics of integrated tribal structures to honor our unities with nature. We long for innocence to sing in us again.

Nature's way is way of abundance, but man has created scarcity that is destroying life through plunder and deception. A better way is to live in accord with "rta" or cosmic rhythm whose cycles may renew and revitalize our perceptions of our relatedness. May it be so!

In such envisioned place, fluidly organized communal structures revere life and allow the participation of each unique genius to flower. Here children are seen for their utter natural beauty and spark of supreme intelligence. Here father and mother, in their adoration of one another, enclose the world with this dynamic loving, having continually recovered their true selves despite their different upbringing. Grandparents and little ones play around trees. Here friends are true not envious. Here people gather to celebrate just because. Here work is but just that which brings more than enough with adequate time for rejuvenation. Here homes are built in keeping with laws of nature and the elements. Here we learn the art of choice and responsibility, where freedom is practice of love. Passion is commitment. We are creative in our diverse ways. Like Cycladic homes woven in rock and mountainside, such tribal structures live in continual innovation for all goodness and with reverence for beauty.

How many layers of stories must be peeled away before we can find truth? And when we have found this truth, how do we know it for having lived with illusions for millennia? How then will we recognize truth of peace and of love that we seek? Will we know it when we come face to face with it? Is it the mirror into which I look daily?

Who are you? Stone, flower, petal, tender satin of petal, a mango, a fig, a date, a pomegranate. A molecule of light, sunrise, quantum of your gaze, breeze that makes music.

Who are you? I am strings of cosmos, song of the underbelly, Avatar, kosmic womb, the great Mother of creation...

Om Bhur Bhuvah Suvah
Tat Savitar Vare Niyam

Bhargo de vasya dhi mahi
Dhiyo yo nah pracho dyaat

The Gayatri Mantra is an homage to the Sun, a million suns, and her brilliance as she enlivens by illumining all that we do and are. This is virtue, is grace.

Of one thing, I feel there is no doubt—we are here on this beauteous Gaia to perfect our loving and our living. What else but this, this perfecting? We learn through opposing forces to create new paradigms. We continue to participate in rituals that will bring us to fullness of our potent humanity to become trans-human. Perhaps, we are not conscious enough...maybe not yet. Such thoughts frequently passage through my mind—have done so since I was a teenager making my way to college across the busy roadways of New Delhi.

What am I here for? And you?

We reach the foot of the mountains at the beach. A few steps above are a temple to Athena and one to Apollo, both overlooking the sea. Broken columns and jagged pieces of rock lie around. Ruins abound in ancient lands. The Indian capital, New Delhi, has been home to nine different kingdoms at different periods in history, and their remains lie sprawled in different areas. It is what makes the city so fascinating; sadly, this metropolis is now an overcrowded mess of broken hopes and dreams, and while young entrepreneurs lead the way in an economic boom that liberates them in some ways, old patterns of behavior keep the city in check; the misery of broken glass and garbage abounds.

Someone calls out to follow the group into the space of the broken temple. This small temple is quite splendid. Fallen

62

pieces seem to make patterns that might resemble constellations; I wonder only because the space pounded by the glare of the June sun must be a mystery to the culture that lost this connection. The location is symbolic; just high enough from sea level, it must have warmed and warned seafarers on their journey.

Further along this hillside, we find a small shack. It is customary for such places of rest to be built in remote areas, just in case someone drops by and needs a place to stay for the night. What a romantic ideal! What comfort abounds in simple folk wisdom! Meeting of human needs—away from shelter, the need for shelter, finding hospitality in a strange place. Here we rest from the glaring sun that has not learned to wear shades. In a short while, my cohorts change into their bathing suits.

Simply marveling at the many hues of layering blues makes everyone excited, and they run into the waves of the ancient Aegean. I hadn't brought my bathing suit for I prefer to swim in the evenings, not under the harsh gaze of a ruddy sun. But, tempted, I wade into the water for a few minutes. The water soothes, the blue so perfectly enchanting. I want to be a mermaid. Deciding to let go, I undress down to my underclothes and succumb to the cooling water. I swim around some rocks and oh! it is all so heavenly. Almost in a flash are gone the rigid walls of academia, the sordid smoggy streets, cultural maxims, fears—everything is washed away. Wild and happy fantasies invade me, all of us. We become naiads, *apsaras*—we are divinity incarnate, but of course. Suddenly, I lapse into fairy tales with one of my cohorts, Nikita. When she laughs, it feels like magic. Her white teeth glint like light over the blue waves. "M*aya*"—Greek word for magic means illusion in Sanskrit. Both have spoken. The world is magical, we are an illusion, and we are real pulsing holograms dancing in time somewhere in spaces or in the in-between spaces. Here we transcend illusion to become real.

I understand what it feels like to be perfecting design, the poem yet unfolding, a poem that never ends. How can I end or you when we each are continually coming into being and time is fluid as dream?

Someone takes pictures of us from the shore. We are on the rocks where foam dances and cannot be shaken like a martini.

Even as I wade back, my toes hit sharp rocks. My feet burn intensely, but I think nothing of it; perhaps it is just a sharp rock and my feet are cut. Little do I know what this "rock" is. It would prove to be a mark of destiny, a bite of reality. But, right now, I swim in dreamscape light dancing in, on and off the rolling waves....

Messages from the Deep...

I hear mermaids singing—waters flowing fish breathing. I wish to be them—naiads, apsaras, elves, fairies... Creatures of divinity of dreams, swallowed by timelines.

I wish to be a mermaid to flow-breathe wisdom of water; dream amid coral and weed, be caressed by primal sounds in this sweet element so salty and sometimes bitter—life's vicissitudes, where weeds float and I so free of pain.

Tears in salt water! Baptized daily anew, I'd swim the world... No boundaries, no visas here—! But wait!

Those big mean eyes of shark shambling and terrible trembles tumble inside me. I stutter, swallow water. Heart stops—I am drowning—And! Biting cold winds scream on my face... spray of memory sparkle million drops of sea foam on my face.

My eyes so suddenly full of salt!

I am bitten and swallowed by seaweed. I do not recall if I yell to be awake... the noise so endless—then everything stops. No more foam...the waves are far away—Safety tastes like this. I am solidity on rock! Such silence that everything recedes in warp space.

Suddenness of clarity in being-ness so enlivens. Dream safely of mermaids, Child. Magazine pages float away in waves of shimmering moonlight.

Sun has dropped from view. I smile. Sages have told me to always smile. Come what may.

Songs haunt from the deep. Songs that baptize us with language: tributaries of inner connections.

A Wooing of Sea Urchins

I finally come out of the water (and maybe to my senses) and limp back to the shack. My toes are swollen and I still think it was a sharp rock. *Ohi!* I have been introduced to the world of sea urchins. My big right toe is marked with eleven love spears; these spikes stay in my toes for three days, after which Zaneta, who works in the hotel, pulls them out with loving determination. She is so very skillful. If this were to happen again to me, I'd like to be near her. For now, needless to say, the walk back up the hill with camera bag and heat and toes with spikes is torturous.

Suddenly, I choose to feel safe and still as I listen to Seamus talk about Homer's *Odyssey*; it provides a metaphor for our trip here, that this trip is just another story, that stories take us into light, into the underworld, as our eternal quest. Stories are quests for answers and, as we wish, happy endings. The fact that some end in sadness and tragedy is just that simple measure that reminds us of the threads of life. The weave is multi-colored and of many dimensions of human thought and emotion. The outcome is never guaranteed, but it may be chosen.

Yes. First a funeral and now this. Offering a piece of limb as a feast for an urchin in the sea not on the street must be a ritual of sacrifice. Okay. I am beginning to understand. I

65

remember my Native American friends who perform the sun dance and offer their flesh for the good of humanity; they gouge bits of flesh from their shoulders even as they dance in the hot Arizona summer as they pray for the people of the land and tribes, lost or dead or forgotten. Of course, the sea urchin and my toes do not have the status of a religious ritual, but it brings me to my silence, reminds me that I can endure—that anything can become a religious experience. If anything, it can make me grow, be strong, practice art of laughter. That is what our parents would have us believe, and for now, this teaching comes in handy. Struggle makes a person strong; sometimes, it can break one. The beliefs we create and are born to live by can come to mean nothing at all. Best to empty—but how? How? Just like how we empty rooms when we move?

The walk back up the hill to the bus is no fun with needles in my toes, the heat with its arrows, the drudge of ancient gravelly dust, with the weight of a Sony PD 150 camera and bag in my arms. I make it. A few tears and great goodness in the history of epic lands. My toes look like a pincushion poked with black dots. The recommended olive oil dabs do nothing to remove the sullen barbs sticking stubbornly to me. I walk on my heels for some days. Nice. I think I did not leave footprints in the sand but those in my heart, well-heeled and well-oiled (!) for a few days.

Tales of Childhood and Ancient Days

In the evening we are treated to a film, *The Cistern* (2001), which is "a dark fairytale about childhood in the light of Greece" in the words of the film's director, Christos Dimas. The film is multi-layered and reveals the fantasies, games, and traumas of childhood in a somewhat magic realism style, one that I aspire to and sometimes use in my stories.

Christos Dimas' baby *The Cistern* is well received by the group, most of whom feel inspired by the fantasy element in the narrative. Based loosely on characters whom he had known in his childhood and events that he had witnessed including the death of two friends in his fantastical growing years, the film incorporates Dimas' own endearing habits in his main character: a child hiding under beds and tables and being part of adult dramas while seemingly uninvolved; child dressed in scuba gear and swimming on his bed. Such elements of fantasy work well woven into the larger story. Parts of the film are obtuse and the ending somewhat unclear as is life in its ambiguities, but the film is, nevertheless, a treat and lesson in style and poignancy.

Seamus suggests we look at how effectively Dimas transposed his childhood memories into this visual narrative. Someone notes he was moved by the juxtaposition and effective use of furniture that seemed almost theatrical. Someone else remarks on the post-modern interpretation of childhood longing in a culture in transition. We are reminded of diverse ways of looking at memory and how it may reveal something hidden at the time of the experiencing. Seamus suggests we make notes of specific childhood events, where truth and falsehood mingled to create confusion. I wonder if, perchance, herein is one source of our ongoing deceptions so we cannot tell the difference.

Lack of safety in communal structures seems to be part of so many lands today as social systems are in fragmentation, awaiting a brutally honest self-evaluation.

This day leaves me in nostalgia, in longing, which seems to be the current theme in my life. Always in longing. The ruins in Karthea bring me to see and know how deeply Greece is buried. The ancient culture with its rites, rituals, and enlivening practices is buried. I am buried. We are all buried. We keep on burying ourselves with layers of words and metaphors, mediated needs leading to slavish consumption.

We keep building over that which we have buried. How deep must excavations go?

Where does the truth lie, especially now when we are buried deeper with televised untruths and the machinations of fear wrought by the powers that be? Where is our poetry? How do we live? On what do we live? On what should we?

Ancient texts tell us that everything is an illusion. We receive the world through our senses, and we must use our mind in order to make sense of the confusion of the senses, in order to bring balance and fortitude in our lives, in order to develop high character. In order to retrieve ourselves from these buried lands, from buried spaces in our own bodies, from the buried loves that haunt us in our idealizations. Perhaps, it is for all the above that Odysseus wandered and Jason lusted after the Golden Fleece. And Rama traveled with his army to bring back his beautiful wife, Sita, a woman of uncommon intelligence who maintained her purity of vision and had the power to refuse Rama after his rejection of her when he gave in to the populace in Ayodhya.

And what do we lust after? In our urban sprawls, marked by postmodern paranoia, chemical trails, allergies, time that is caught in fragmented cellular panic of having to get so much done, so that we walk further away from ourselves to seek ourselves. It seems, too, in my life that I have wandered away from my own idealizations, sometimes lured away, sometimes seduced by a different idea or temptation only to find that it was not "my thing"; then to find that these served to bring me back closer to my true self, which is still unfolding. It never ceases, like the river, which ends in eternal seas. I am reminded of Emily Dickinson's poem:

> "The Sea said 'Come' to the Brook –
> The Brook said 'Let me grow' –
> The Sea said 'Then you will be a Sea –
> I want a Brook – Come now'!
>
> The Sea said 'Go' to the Sea –
> The Sea said 'I am he/
> You cherished' – 'Learned Waters –
> Wisdom is stale – to Me'"

The Brook in her wisdom notes with dignity that she'd rather move on or else lose her identity, while "The Sea" Brook notes is becoming stale with wisdom.

68

While sages, teachers, mystics note that meditations are silent journeys within, I wonder if wandering away and without may be journeys within. We are catapulted out only to boomerang back in, deeper than before, sometimes more painfully so in order to find the joy. Then there are other ways of travel to move slowly and mindfully towards the many chambers of the inner heart.

But in these modern times, we want everything now, we want everything to be convenient, and if we do not get what we want immediately, we develop issues and complexes. Perhaps what we have not considered is that we need a simple way to perceive time, space, and our relationship with them and with each other.

How shall our needs be met? For the simple ways we used to know, ways we have always known now have the veneer of complexity. Why did we forget them over eons of human culture? Are we returned to a past where we had forgotten something or are we here to cleanse this dimension of its sordid mishaps and our limitations in this dimension? Traumas of all our pasts have brought us to an impasse.

It feels as though we have lost something and must now re-create ways to communicate with one another with simplicity and patience. This surely is the path to revealing ourselves as the beloved. Then we may joyfully be present to enjoy presence. Our days now become filled with work—this is not solace but pressure. Some work today has lost soul.

An Indian mystic had noted that people spend so much time, energy, patience, skill working hard to go to the moon, but he can go there in an instant and return. This is more than astral travel. Do scientists who are enlightened know this to be true?

I would love to travel to the moon in an instant. With you. I close my eyes.

Let me swallow the moon
to share with you
supernal light...

69

Let me sing a tune
or two and see a rose
at edge of night...

how she might glance
this passing moon

goldenish trail
kiss of delight...

Let me simply be ensconced
in a bed of red-hued rose petals

sip rose mulled
in camphor wine

"Fables should be taught as fables, myths as myths, and miracles as poetic fantasies. To teach superstitions as truths is a most terrible thing. The child mind accepts and believes them, and only through great pain and perhaps tragedy can he be in after years relieved of them."

~ Hypatia

Chapter 4 ~ Art, Life, & Alchemy

It is no accident that we've focused on Homer these last few days. Today is June 16, the day of Ulysses' meanderings as interpreted by Ireland's beloved James Joyce, who also celebrates his birthday on this day. So we, too, meander, in and out of sensations and perceptions. We sit in a story circle and share our experiences before leaving for the monastery where we will listen to Katerina Evangelakou speak about her movie *Think it Over* (2002), which we shall watch in the evening.

The Greek Orthodox Monastery of Katariani for the Assumption of the Virgin Mary is set on the top of a cliff, which tapers down into the wide openly gasping sea. Greece has the landscape of my dreams where rugged rocky cliffs end in blue seas. So much beauty in having all the elements solidly in their place all together! The strength and stoicism of earth and rock, the flow and passion of the waters, the sweet serenity of breezes, the fire that moves all into being and balance with the challenge of keeping all in balance, neither too hot, nor too cold. Our eternal search for balance often takes us out of it. If we only remembered that as dynamic beings, we move in and out of balance perpetually—in rhythmic process and in flow—we might, perhaps, be less flustered at finding ourselves in discord in a moment.

It is interesting that all of us with cameras arrive at new locations and become busy little image carnivores. Gone are all sensibilities as we become focused behind the lens and wonder at the beauty around us. Do we miss the experiencing of such beauty when we capture it all for some future consumption, which must necessarily be indirect and incomplete, for the minute cellular thrills cannot be felt again but only remembered for delayed pleasure? Memories are powerful presences in our subconscious; they can even lash out like monsters.

As I take pictures of the landscape, I see an elderly man look at me and then at his wife. I put away the camera wondering if he is offended by this intrusion. I wander into the *kafé*, to the toilet, then return, and see his wife coming up to me all smiles, so many smiles. She hugs me. She is very excited to meet me. This older lady named "Vara" is sweet and passionate and won't let go of me. I am a bit charmed and a bit on guard at her effusiveness. Through gestures, I let her know I cannot stay long as I am in a class over there, under the trees on the steps of the monastery. Not an English speaker, she understands what I am conveying and nods smiling. One of my cohorts is near me; I ask her to take pictures of us. Vara smiles, then laughs; her daughter, Iokaste, comes and poses with us; her husband, Zosimos, smiles indulgently. *Vara* is short for Velissaria; in Sanskrit, *"vara"* means promise. I do not know the meaning in Greek.

Gradually, I extricate myself feeling a bit overwhelmed at this display of affection—I am a stranger, after all—and rejoin the group. The session with Katerina concludes and after a quick walk around, we are hustled into the bus to return to our hotel. At that moment, Vara comes up to me and gives me a slab of chocolate. Her daughter translates that she brought me the chocolate because she likes me. In the meanwhile, Seamus is concerned that I am keeping the bus waiting. He yells that they will leave me here if I do not hurry. What can I do?

I cannot leave her so abruptly. But we hurriedly exchange addresses and I leave. Her husband shouts after me, "You are a good woman...you will come back and live here." Prophecies abound in old lands. It must be the call of the spirit in some way. I am in wonder at the kindness of people I meet where I travel. Some people think I am Greek. I have not come to live here. Perhaps, I already have lived here. This much is true. Perhaps, living many lives makes us time travelers in awareness.

There's much to think about, to feel, to know.

First, I must reflect on Katerina's work, for the discussion of her film and her aesthetic have already taken place at this monastery. She has talked about her film career and her philosophy of filmmaking. Her focus, she has noted, is on editing for that is what makes the film. "Don't say more than you absolutely have to," is her credo. We like her finely designed posters and listen to her narrative on how the project was completed.

While in the circle with Katerina, Seamus, the joyful facilitator, has passed out blurbs about people killed on September 11, 2001. We create brief narratives inspired by the information given us. There has been a creative outpouring as the writers among us are stirred to make up stories in an instant. We reflect on shadows in our psyche that would create such horror. The event was almost a year ago; little did we know then what more would sweep the globe with horror and darkness. Here we feel sated by the light around and arising in us.

Later in the evening, we watch Katerina Evangelakou's *Think it Over* (2002). A nicely made touching film leads to a conflicting discussion about what constitutes a woman's film. My group is torn over wanting to classify texts according to gender and to see them as universal/humanistic. Yet, this film might easily be included in the curriculum for a course on Women's Studies whereas Dimasis' film could not—he had noted his film is a dark metaphoric fairy tale about childhood set "in the light of Greece." *Think it Over* explores the life of a woman and her relationships and how she may create her life.

In Evangelakou's film, a woman turns forty. She is unmarried, pregnant by a man thirteen years her junior, and she wonders if he will show up to be with her or not. As she leaves her friend's salon, she trips on the sidewalk. She remains lying on her back until the end of the film, which is developed in flashbacks that narrate her life story: her life as a daughter and the oldest of three sisters. It is interesting to note that she is primed for university honors, but does not take her exam.

Somehow she remains indifferent to being left out. In a strange romantic entanglement, she takes care of her mother's friend's son and becomes involved with him. Finding herself pregnant, she doubts his commitment. In the end, loose threads come together in a marriage of wit and irony that makes the drama mildly appealing only for the "good" ending. The young man arrives after all, and they end up together. The film concludes with the protagonist on the beach reading and looking on at her four- to five-year-old son at play, making patterns in the sand with the father.

On the beach, she reads a book about mathematics to discover the mathematical formation of our world. It seems to be a particularly Greek preoccupation—this desire to proclaim to the world that we are all connected mathematically. That conceptual math provides us with the framework to understand our reality—physical, spiritual, and metaphysical. Somehow we arrive at the Golden Mean—a set of numbers that defines our upward movement in a divine spiral. This knowledge offers a sense of certainty to some of our lives and, with this, purpose and, maybe, even an ability to manifest beauty in our created destinies.

I remember Konstantine, the tall gaunt waiter at the *kafé* in the Plaka. He, too, had spoken of math, but he couldn't get me to go with him because of mathematics, or anything else, even though it spoke of our harmony. Now it feels important to return to Evangelakou's struggle to make her art. She has spoken much about the struggle of the artist to create amid financial and commercial difficulties is like any human struggle. So, she notes, we always turn our attention to this in our societies, for living is an art in itself and the artist's struggle is a metaphor for others to define their own life path.

We discuss the role of the artist to highlight social concerns and human ones too. As artists how do we select issues of concern to us as social beings: women's issues, education systems, aging and disease, poverty, religion or science or spirituality—they are all local and global. Our co-evolution is inter-related: what webs we do weave that leave us perplexed and, at times, in wonder; sometimes this uncertainty adds to our concerns about art's purpose.

Such conflicts in me always left me to conclude that art cannot be separate from social needs—that we have a right and duty to transform the world with our art, to assist its evolution or transformation with awareness. There is no other way. Perhaps, this makes my work somewhat didactic but not always; the archetypal, ecstatic, primitive, and colorful can also enliven.

Making art is a journey. Taking a journey is an art.

I wonder about the hidden motives of Odysseus and Jason in their quest. I wonder, too, of the women they mated; while Penelope, warding off seducers and suitors, waited for Odysseus, Medea, medicine woman, guided Jason to safety and to the prize, only to be betrayed at a later time, but who also committed a heinous crime. Now a recreation and re-interpretation of old myths tell us of a metaphysical significance as in the travels of the hero to find himself: love and self-awareness are both motivator and prize. The struggle of the artist is that of the hero to create and co-create, reveal conflicts, wherein all issues are of concern to all humanity.

Dilemmas, conflicts, and uncertainty are woven in the journey that makes us artists if we are not so already. What if we began with having and knowing that which is self-evident or hidden: love? That the meaning of life is to understand and to share love—this elusive and complex state of being. Is this not what every story, song, and poem is ultimately about? Why this absence then of that essential love and loving principle, which is the matrix of the universe? If we are in search of it, we know what the "it" is. Don't we?

Or is love a mystery we cannot attain or appropriate? But it is a feeling arising from intense awareness of our unities beyond limitations. Most of our lives seem to focus on struggle and drama. If we did not have to struggle so, what stories would we create that would remind us of what we are capable of becoming, once we have become love?

Living is an art.

Struggle we do, whether we are artists or not. Today, that struggle seems to be how to get money for work that is of value to all of us. How grossly unbalanced is a system that provides for and makes possible high-tech, special effects films that can lack story, depth, and passion. When millions are poured into the industry that is Hollywood, which churns out similar stuff over and over again, the question may be asked where does the responsibility lie? Is it in the audience who are not hungry to express their inherent greatness or in the makers of these stories who churn them out for the big money? But there is a hunger and it has been trailing and lifting its head again and again.

No wonder then that enlightened writers and directors in the film world have turned their attention to developing stories that make a difference, that awaken. Perhaps this new awareness will lead to greater depth in content, with stories and characters who are passionate in their quest for profound transformation and that appeal to all ages with a call to inner passion and purpose. The aesthetic of film allows for wonderment in the process of unfolding: a journey of mind, heart, and psyche. It is time for us to grow up.

For too long, we've been deluged with special effects and characters that lack passion; violence and sex are not passion. But sexuality is passion when expressed with restraint and flow and power and beauty in a resonant field of love. The present depiction is of both violence and sex as merely physical expressions of suppressed energy. Spirituality is not a new theme: not in film, art, or sexual expression. People are just re-awakening to it in these modern times even as darkness of prurience has taken over.

Passion really is an expression of deep commitment to something—an idea, person, cause, or endeavor. Passion is also expressed in containment—it is also about a journey of unfolding vision, wherein the hero/protagonist believes in something bigger than herself. This is an epic experience. Respect for universal law, nature and cosmos is profound; this makes Odysseus' journey a passionate one. When he errs and falls to delusions, he must learn to expunge himself of his darkness.

Furthermore, the journey, Odysseus' journey and ours too now, is a familiar archetype of change and growth for the attainment of wonder. From the churning emerges purified pats of butter. The pure and impure separate; gold and poison are revealed. Such a revelation illumines. We are left with a valuable lesson: elixir attained by alchemy. Thusly stories within stories within stories are but building materials in the larger cosmic design, the web of possibilities.

In the discussion that follows in our story-writing circle, we are reminded by Seamus, our facilitator, of the stories that surround us in the news, advertising, careless chitchat, the endless diatribe, passing of time as newscasters interpret news with feelings. Human experiences, joys, and motivations are continually dissected. He points out the negating influence of such stories in the media. The vacuity, the senselessness that has become the plight of modern man! Do we really want those to filter into our subconscious?

In the middle of all this, I recall, of course, that the highlight at the monastery was my meeting with Vara. Tiny moments make a story meaningful, for in humanized element is the touch of spirit, the flowering of spiritual potential, the human in its greatest strengths. When we smile at each other, we connect with our heartstrings.

Somewhere at the back of my mind, I wonder if I had come to Greece to free parts of me buried in the day-to-day shuffle, for such meetings as the one with Vara and others nurture and trigger me. I also say to the group that I came here to liberate myself. Seamus comments on this strange intention of mine. At Delphi the important words are "Know thyself!" Somewhere in the center, the east and west meet. Self-knowledge is liberation: realizing one's self is both impetus and effect of freeing one self, even from the dregs of living and from various notions of self.

My year-old dream of the labyrinth comes to mind. In the dream, I'd said to my father that if the leaders of India and Pakistan entered this labyrinth from two ends, they would eventually meet in the middle. When they find themselves in the center, they would magically resolve all conflicts once and for all, for they would face each other's humanness. Once in the center, where else can one go? Well.

Perhaps in the center they will laugh. But the labyrinth is key here for its pattern suggests a path to the center where lie secrets that are sacred; in the presence of the sacred, is there conflict or simply a silent brimming of spontaneous joy? Does this create anew or annihilate totally?

And knowledge of the sacred can be dangerous; hence, much of such wisdom has been kept from the masses and used for internecine quarrels. This must be the un-love expressed by human limitation, which seeks to monetize lack and limitation. Real love should free us, not entrap us. And the sacred should remind us of our sovereignty, and one another's. How can we then war with one another?

We are each a center of the universe, each unique and singular.

Alchemy of Center...

Centers keep shifting

*There are many levels of Being &
Nothingness—There is no one real feeling
 or state or ecstasy.*

*I am a conglomerate of conflicting emotions, layers
upon layers upon windowed layers: Soul forces, lights,
shadows, metaphors.*

*I am tradition, home, joy... I am pathos.
I am sometimes awnings of meaninglessness.*

*From whence do I come, but from home,
eternal and sometimes ungraspable?*

*I am space and spaces, treetops, tree fall, rainbows,
darkness; I am my own shelter, my caves, my eaves.*

I steal myself from my Self—return myself to Light.

*I, too, am a child of god—light divine.
I am joys, love, eternal love, eternally!*

*When I fall, I am reminded that all I have to share with
the world is Love. This center.*

This love transcends both pain and pleasure. Nothing else is!

There's nothing like good warm comfort food to bring one's scattered selves back to center, to community. We return to important matters: communion. To celebrate life is so simple, truly simple. Sometimes, this return begins in the belly.

I seem to have made Taverna Afri my favorite haunt—they serve terrific *spanakopita* (spinach and feta wrapped in filo) and *kalamari* with rice. Even so, I find my palate enjoys a small range of foods. Flavors are not as varied as in Indian cooking, and my tastes remain at mildly savory or spicy to somewhat sweet. One day, the lady of the restaurant invites me into the kitchen to show me around. I admit I have myself cooked *gemista* (bell-peppers stuffed with flavored rice) and it hasn't turned out badly; an Indian variation is to stuff it with savory potatoes.

I look at the women looking at me. The women always hug and kiss me when I visit. They make me feel I am a part of them; though somewhat exotic, we also connect because of our ancient history. Maybe this is why each moment is a joy—community in passing.

We come out and I find a nice seat. In a moment this sweet other-worldly Regas, an Albanian immigrant, comes to take my order. He is shy in front of my camera. But one day before I leave, he isn't able to escape my lens. I eat lunch with Brady, one of my cohorts, and the bunch. With us are Ona and Sylvia. Regas serves us. I brandish my old Nikon, its leather case in tatters. He laughs shyly, his sweet curls framing his flirtatious dark eyes. The inevitable happens; his image is finally impressed upon my film.

youthful eyes glow
even seas have curls
     desire...

81

Blending of Landscapes and Illusions

On June 17, we travel to Koundouros, the village of windmills. Breaking from the rest of the island, at Koundouros, the architecture loses its charm as it looks imported, intrusive, uninteresting, designed for tourists, or something built just for convenience as in many places worldwide. So I feel a little bit disappointed, but the beach is terrific. It spreads in shallow waves for quite a bit. It's an easy swim. I have forgotten all about the sea urchins.

The spreading beach under the waves reminds me of Chandipur-at-sea in Orissa, India, which I visited with my family years ago when I was a teen. Set near the tropics and covered with palm trees, Chandipur beach spread for a long while before the sands began to sink deeper into the continental shelf. Koundouros takes me back to this precious memory.

Everyone is feeling ravenous, so the driver brings out hampers of food. Our picnic consists of cheese sandwiches and salad, a simple repast for this short trip. We return to Kea and to our rooms. The rest of the afternoon lazily floats in the heat. Some return to the waters around the hotel; others rest in their rooms.

On our last evening here on Kea, we watch Preston Sturges' *The Palm Beach Story* (1942), somewhat like Shakespeare's *A Comedy of Errors,* wherein at the end everything is put right and all couples are partnered appropriately. Nice to watch something seemingly silly, but we know how much goes in to make it so all is clear. It takes supreme intelligence to be effectively and wildly funny—the comedic illumines life's struggles and shows a way to resolution. It also takes smartness to offer slapstick, which can be painful; note the physical violence in films of Laurel and Hardy and others.

Life must be a carnival—how we forget this axiom as we get wrapped up in our tensions, replaying of our traumas, and minor humdrum tirades at the day's irritations. So we fantasize to experience freedom, to commune with others, to find that the world is truly topsy-turvy and not even-tempered as we would expect or want it to be. Indeed to know the human spirit is to celebrate it. Seamus, the facilitator, reminds us that carnival celebrates freedom, fantasy, and community. No wonder then that I live for the most part in my many fantasies, like Alice in a dance with the Mad Hatter in Wonderland. No wonder that my chosen natural genre and style are fantasy, magic realism, and the ecstatic. Perhaps it's easier for me to speak to and about many levels of thought all at once. So we make stories, a network of stories, where no one dare say, "Off with her head!" Everything is everything just as it is.

Living is a celebration.

Kea provides many opportunities to commune. We eat, we sing, we dance—such are the beginnings of human stories. We begin with an "other" in our sharing and, at the end of it, there is no "other." We have become the "other"; then there is a separating of skins so that we can return to commune again and again.

Seamus loves to tell us that Greeks and the Balkan people know what it means to party—you never tell someone when a party is to end; this happens only in the US. Seamus tells us of his friend who was insulted by an invitation to a party that stipulated the hour of its beginning and its end, 7-10 p.m. How can you say when a party is to end? *Tsk tsk.* He refused to go, for in the Balkans, partying and communing is to eat, drink, make merry until the wee hours. Impose no limits.

Add to Balkan sensibility this—they party after the bombing. Humor is the order of the day in stressful times. There is no other way to deal with the vagaries of life. It is the genre of comedy that celebrates triumph. It is triumph that brings us a sense of joy; hence, it is comedic. Comedy is a sigh of relief after the beating, the hammering and the killing and seeing that we have come through it all. Comedy is an attitude. Comedy is a flourish of the human spirit to endure the travails of destiny, the ache of the past, the wonder of and in us all. It is a belly full of chortles at our errors. Humanizing elevates us.

Does tragedy not do the same? If it ends in a triumph, does this not elevate us for having survived? The spirit has endured and has emerged with new knowledge or remembered knowledge. Bloodshed is followed by a rebirth, not just a death. "There is no death!" the protagonist had exuberantly noted in *Never on a Sunday*—the children had gotten up and walked away. Even protagonists may fantasize about life. We are the protagonists of our epic story.

Tragic drama suggests a reflection on our own foibles and lessons on what human actions we must change or transcend in order to evolve. We live with illusions that we create. Let us not die with illusions, nor allow them to kill us.

Leaving Kea

This is the last night at Kea. There are fourteen at dinner at Ianni's restaurant near the boats. Men at a nearby table celebrate our group's wild sense of play. They ply the creative writers with *retsina*. Ianni, owner of the restaurant, and I chat. He offers me *retsina*; instead, I ask for tea. He takes me into the kitchen and wraps up some mountain tea for me to take back and makes me a hot cup of this beverage.

Again someone celebrates my origins, tells me of his days in South Africa. Ianni with a balding pate speaks of discrimination he had suffered there. He remembers the Indian restaurant he would frequent, where his Indian friend would pack him meals to go. It was unlawful for a non-Afrikaner to use such public facilities. He is grateful for his Indian friend who would bring food to this "lonely Greek at the rear door of the kitchen." His eyes water as he tells me of his experience. We smile in understanding...a flavor of silence rises.

Eventually, we step out of the kitchen, and he introduces me to his wife, Thespina. I take pictures. She remembers seeing me on my first evening on this island when my cohorts and I walked past her one evening in search of a meal. Smiling, she gives me the packet of mountain sage tea Ianni had prepared. I still have it wrapped in foil in my kitchen drawer: a symbol of communion I am choosing to not consume; I keep it so I am reminded of tender connections on this island, vestiges of moments that return for a caress.

It is the 18th of June, a Tuesday. I call my grandmother each year on this day for it is my grandfather's birthday; he has been gone for a long while. This time I am unable to call. A little twinge of guilt shifts my heart for a moment; then I choose to be pragmatic, I excuse myself, even though I don't feel quite so good about it.

On our last day in Kea, we have to be on time. In fact, we leave early to take the only boat out of Kea before the boatmen's strike begins as scheduled. It is a strange irony that the strike is announced late at night. We could have been stranded on Kea for days had this shipping company broken an agreement and shut down sooner than the scheduled hour. Luck is with us, but some fellow travelers groan at the idea of going back to a city. We will have but one day in Delphi, and we must visit the grand Oracle for a lesson in knowing ourselves. We must not miss the bus that will take us to Delphi from Lavrion. There is but one boat and we cannot miss this either.

Before we reach the port of Lavrion, I meet my new "friends" from the monastery again. The father, Zosimos, recognizes and waves to me. We have a fairly long conversation: The daughter, Iokaste, her partner, Otis, and I, with the father insisting that I should live in Greece. He says he feels strongly that I will not return to Los Angeles. I laugh. Who knows? Anything can happen. We plan on connecting again in Athens. Vara, who has been sitting down below in the closed area is again enthusiastic and affectionate. She won't let go of me from her tight embrace; I am trying to protect my dark glasses from being smashed between her bosom and mine.

What a conflict! Love and eye-piece.

Considering I am almost blind without sunglasses—too much fire for my eyes—I choose to protect my twenty-dollar sunglasses. Lovingness is always welcome. There's never enough poured out even though there's plenty to go around.

I wonder that we have made it an art to hold in our innermost feelings lest we reveal too much who we truly are, lest we are not understood, lest....

seagull
shatters sky
into feathers

clouds over sun-swept sea
sail on by
each a shape-shifter

my eyes blink
in the sea-full breeze
noises of the boat
people in heat

cool beers in hand
laughter competing with
drone of roaring engines

so much love
boat will not sink

how can it
with this much laughter

"If cattle and horses, or lions, had hands, or were able to draw with their feet and produce the works which men do, horses would draw the forms of gods like horses, and cattle like cattle, and they would make the gods' bodies the same shape as their own."

~ Xenophanes

Chapter 5 ~ Discovering Delphi and *"Ekfrastikotita"*

As we approach Delphi, I am reminded that Otis, a self-styled New-Ager, in the boat from Kea had said that the Oracle always gave two answers so that people make their choice and are thus responsible for their destiny and path. Of course, this is wise or stupid-cunning in a way—*coutoponeros*? —for some think the Oracles were but women affected by the vapors of the hot spring.

Are the Oracles smarter than the *rishis* and astrologers who imposed control by rigid adherence to their own morality and thereby subjugated people? Especially women who surrendered their knowingness and placed their faith in these sages and were, in turn, controlled by predictions and strictures, thereby losing their own sense of self and destiny. Perhaps these dynamic affected women adversely who became willing believers and lost their power for generations, while their inner knowing became squashed and power was lost to external unbridled authority. Together, men and women created such illusions and became controlled by them. It is disconcerting to think of what cultural norms can do to a life supposed to have been lived and loved gloriously.

The drive to Delphi is long and arduous, and our driver Bobi is careful and pleasant. Before we get on our way, we stop at Sounion for a short visit—the temple to Poseidon arrests us in its solitariness overlooking the great waters. The place is closed at this hour, so we content ourselves with the shops and visit to the restrooms. We spend minutes *ooh-ing* and *ah-ing* over postcards of various ancient sites. But here, too, sex images sell; however, they lack erotic appeal. Steamy images and manipulations are displayed with an unseemly candor, placed in a way to draw your eyes towards them, rather than the ones of the temple or those that speak of a historical mythical significance; the penis, whose drive has conquered, slaughtered, and plundered many a virgin land has, in its own way, influenced our history and mythology.

These images are brazen manipulations inviting my self-righteous voice to suggest that the *Shiva Linga*, cosmic phallus or egg as prime co-creator, is usually more aesthetically offered. But prurient man has also cheapened himself; male gaze has also demeaned masculinity, which could be represented with more grace for it has its own beauty. These postcards cheapen virility of the Greek gods and of Michelangelo's *David*. The same is done to women's breasts on cheap postcards, aprons, t-shirts, underclothes; all are unappealing. Such graphic forms of cheap vulgarization are sadly present in all lands.

Something in people's relationship with sex and sexuality weakens them to their own sensuality. Instead of claiming it, they are impelled to decry it, to make fun of it, to objectify the human body and individual organs, to separate themselves from what is essentially beautiful, for it is life-endowing, life-enriching, life-balancing, enhancing the stuff that makes life vital and joyful. When people diminish the power of a person in partnership and in loving, they cease to recognize their own worth. So much shame when we can celebrate and mutually accept the very stuff that makes life! Why is it that cultures worldwide cannot reconcile beauty with life giving?

The bell rings; time is now; we must leave. The drive to Delphi is long, and the day becomes warmer by the second. This promises to be a hot journey during which we could lose the self and find the soul. Perhaps. I reflect on the male gaze, how all are fallen in its traps, how we may instead arise with sacred connection in our hearts.

Ekho, our very knowledgeable and sprightly guide, meets us at Delphi where it is insurmountably, insufferably hot. Everyone seems to be sinking/melting in the heat. Bearing this torture, we find the museum splendid, as is

90

everything else here in this mountain town. It is cooler inside. My gratitude rises in appreciation.

Back at the ruins, I am confronted with a magnificent display of religious and political icons and artifacts of antiquity. Commerce has always flourished in matters of the soul. Nothing has changed. The soul or the spirit is always up for sale. We live in a material world—Madonna sang of it. I recognize how clever is this woman to have deftly soaked up material culture to her advantage. This is a powerful lesson to some of us who are so immersed in a spiritual process that aspects of living elude us; I wonder if such indulgence might be a fear of full immersion or of fulfillment in all aspects of living, or even a denial of one's various attributes when no part is separate from the other; material and spiritual life mirror each other.

At Delphi too image sells, as it does everywhere, in places of worship and even in Vatican City. All churches, mosques, temples are built by the rich and controlled by the powerful wealthy, while some poor pray for wealth and weep with a religiosity that does not change material conditions, which languish in decay. Poverty, unhygienic conditions, starvation, homelessness, war...the list is endless. Too many etceteras equal excesses leading to a lack of quality of life.

In how many ways are people controlled, especially the poor. Promise of spiritual salvation is one. New Age spirituality is a re-evaluation of eternal wisdom with practices taught in workshops that are far too expensive for most people who remain stuck to the words of priests who maintain power in their institutions, which hinders spiritual freedom. While this gives some hope, might it be a continuation of an old message popularized in new garb? The difference, however, is that anyone can be a self-styled guru— even teacher-ship is up for sale. What kind of wisdom is this? Must anyone with revelatory experiences become a guru? Pop culture's near-falsified democracy of spirituality, a New Age cyberspace where anyone can be a guru or oracle is prime commodity.

Schools, too, offer a kind of control that does not enhance excellence but encourages and educates mediocrity of spirit. I feel triggered by the chaos around us. At the same time, I wonder how to drop my old ways into the dust of Greece.

I take pictures of Athena, of Aphrodite, of the other gods who rest in stony splendor on pedestals designed to carry their weight. Sculptured friezes tell stories. Beautifully fine carvings are sublime. We wonder at the artistry and the devotion to creating beauty. It is so important to bring this quality back in our environments and make beauty a cause, beautify our environments, see beauty as a path to peace, which it, indeed, is. I do not know that in a few years, we will lose the magnificent Bamian statues of the Buddha in Afghanistan to acts of terror. Intention to cause such destruction is never sanctioned by any god. It cannot be. Leaders are blinded by an arrogance that closes to them the doors of heaven, place of the heart; naturally, being blind, they do not see this.

We are told not to use cameras inside the museum. Ekho is vibrant, quick-witted, lovely, and plump. Attentive and engaging, she ends sentences with a question. A Delphic child? I learn that the word for sister is *Delphus* and brother, *Delphos*—Delphi is the womb. So that which springs from the womb is either *Delphus or Delphos*. There is also the cosmic egg, which is conceptually similar to the Indian cosmic phallus, the *shivalinga,* revered as symbol of generative source. I remember, too, my drawing of a similar cosmic egg encircled by a serpent rising. It is exciting to see interconnections between symbols and motifs in stories of different cultures. These journeys into the collective unconscious intrigue and thrill me. Sometimes, I take such symbiotic moments for granted. I ought to pay careful attention. I could remove my own ignorance.

After the museum visit, we thank Ekho for her wonderful presence and leave the place of fallen boulders, Omphalos, trees in the hazy heat. We proceed to the town of Delphi and check in at the hotel, walk to a restaurant for a story circle, and I snack again on *spanakopita.* Naturally, I feel better after eating.

We walk then on the arterial street of the small town. At almost each shop where I have a conversation with the shopkeepers, I learn that the late Indian Prime Minister Indira Gandhi had visited Delphi and their shop. One of the shopkeepers tells me Mrs. Gandhi had said she would write to him, but a few months after her visit in 1984, she was assassinated. Another man has a 50-rupee note tacked on the wall; he is proud of this souvenir. Many shopkeepers do not spend the very first note they make in the day—receiving this money is like breaking a fast and, in business, this exchange becomes a gift, a promise of more to come, so that first note is not used for exchange. Folk wisdom. Good for business. Manifestation.

I remember that with my first salary, I had bought my mother and my father a gold chain each. Honor not commerce.

In one store, I speak to Yorgos T., the proprietor, who is eager to converse. He asks me if I am a teacher. I say "yes" and wonder aloud how he came to that observation. He says it's because of the kinds of questions that I ask him. He then looks at me and says that there's something about my eyes that is "*ekfrastikotita*." I ask what it means. He is effusive in his explanation but cannot quite say; I get the idea that it means expressive. Yet he is not quite satisfied with my choice of the word. It's more than that, he insists. He says that he looks at me and then stops at my eyes ... it's "*ekfrastikotita*." I like the sound of it, resisting the temptation to be carried away by images that flood my mind; will I see in my eyes what he sees? I wish he does not mean the killing eyes of Medusa, but I learn that *ekfrastic* poetry is one developed from photos. Perhaps expression that leads to another expression or arising thereof, hence *ekfrastikotita*!

Eyes that invoke! The provocateur comes to life. A glance is powerful as innuendo, for it can open up a whole new world of possibilities and narrative.

I enter another store to help petite and dark-haired Dede find a turquoise necklace, and there I meet Dionysia and her husband. Dionysia is a maker of copper crocheted belts, baskets, unusual designs of jewelry. The complexity of this copper weaving is remarkable. I buy a beautiful pair of silver earrings from her—it is set with a white stone from Mt. Parnassus. She gives me a happy discount. In the meantime, her husband is on the phone with his brother in San Diego, where wild summer fires rage. He tells me he has no desire to travel. He loves it here in Delphi. Truly, the view is spectacular in this mountain town. Why should he go anywhere far? Why should he go to California? He laughs. There are no fires here in Delphi.

I go back to the hotel to bring my camera. I like to take pictures of people I meet. Buildings by themselves remain innocuous—one building is like another...postcards not chosen carefully so they lack a personal touch. But in these pictures, people smile. They look at you deeply with their eyes—perhaps, giving rise to *ekfrastic* poems. In English, "ekphrastic." Go, find in a picture what is not there.

On Our Way to Thessaloniki

We are to leave early June 19th morning for Levadia to take the train to Katerina so we can take the bus to Thessaloniki. I am downstairs in the café for breakfast. Seamus is there too, serving himself tea. He has already gone on his daily five-mile run around town and is ready to go. Small breakfast, lots of tea, and I am ready. I still have my hat with the large brim; somehow, I feel that I might lose it. We get to the bus waiting at the end of the street. Fellow traveler Martin and I manage to practice some sun salutations, while Laura videotapes us on the pavement in the down dog. A dog comes smiling and wagging to sniff us. This marks the end of the yoga session. The bus is loaded. We depart. Our Yugoslav bus driver, Bobi, is his cheery self.

In Levadia, we drive in search of the train station around blocked streets, then return to the original road and find it is not blocked as Bobi had earlier thought it would be. We reach the station and have a one-hour wait for our train. This means it is a photo opportunity and time for *kafé nero*, of course, and a visit to the toilets. Eastern-style toilets make some crinkle their noses, but I know the toilets are not so dirty here as I have found to be in India from my travels there. Here they call them Turkish toilets, and these are commonly used in Russia as well. According to yogic interventions, these toilets are more effective for peristalsis, for colonic movement, but we all prefer the comfort of Western toilets, perhaps so we can read books and newspapers in private.

Fellow writers Sean, Annie and Miriam star in a commercial for a product named SLUT; I forget what the product is that they created for this enactment. The name is adequate. Jimmy, a happy-go-lucky film enthusiast, directs and shoots this short, which we will view at the Hotel Plaka in Athens some days later.

Finally, the train arrives; we ascend into what is going to be an interesting four hours. We reminisce of sweet moments at Sounion when Jimmy had understood that he was in search of something special and that it is inside of him; therefore, he didn't have to travel far. He had seen the light within. It warmed my heart to see him lose the shadows on his face and replace it with peace. He glowed gently. It is moments such as these that remind us of simple truths, thereby making our connecting special.

What of the shadows on my face?

Traveling in the heat with relative strangers is also challenging. We are each being tested in various ways. Little irritations creep in. Boundaries are being tested, and we are making contact. The subject of boundaries is especially significant in relating for we push boundaries when we reveal ourselves. I come to understand boundaries not merely as limits, which we may not cross but touch so we make contact. If we shy away from such limits, we do not make contact and remain in isolation. We do not relate. Here we practice relating in our own ways, opening up as and when we can. It is not always easy. We cannot always be in agreement and in harmony—conflict is part of growth. Sometimes, boundaries are about learning who we each are, then understanding our self.

In the train, our boundaries are tested even further. It's a matter of seating and remaining seated or giving up the seat to the one assigned a particular seat. Ricky, Seamus, and I are in one compartment. Ricky and I interview Seamus who then leaves to check on other people. Someone enters the compartment and wants us to vacate our seats because she is assigned those. So we do. In the meanwhile, Seamus returns and we move to the other carriage, most of which is assigned to us privileged writers. So there is a seating shuffle from Levadia. Finally, we settle in but not without being told by one young Greek woman that we should never have gotten up and relinquished our seats. We smile and nod; being foreigners and guests of this beauteous land, we wished to not create unpleasantness in any situation.

The journey continues without further ado, except for a lost filming opportunity. How could I have recorded such a happening?

Train Reaction...

People are seated in their seats in one carriage. PeaceMan enters with headphones and a seeming don't care expression, bobbing his head to the music; he looks casually at all the people and walks out to another carriage.

Bobo and Marko are happily seated by a window, when they see people enter their carriage and look around at the numbers on the seats. They try to look unconcerned, but are a little nervous. Dinko is a heavyset guy with a fierce appearance. He eyes the new fellows with disdain and as they come closer, he pulls a hat over his face and slumps down with a "do not disturb" aura around him. Cheekoo and Mikoo come straight towards Bobo and Marko and insist on having their seats. Bobo and Marko, after some negotiating, decide to get up and go to the next carriage where they have assigned seats. Probably.

They enter the next carriage, stand around looking despondent. The train stops and three people get out. This is the chance that Bobo and Marko have been waiting for; they finally have a seat. Nico and Vasi enter the carriage. Nico walks to Bobo and demands his seat—it is assigned to Nico, but Bobo won't get up. In the meanwhile, sitting at the far end of the carriage is Bubba, our PeaceMan—a '60's throwback peacenik with blond dreads (dregs?). He looks out of the window with a glazed expression. He is clearly involved with his music and his fantasies.

Nico, frustrated, leaves the carriage and walks to the next one. We follow him into the carriage where, after some surveillance, he finds a seat and plops down. He sets his bag between his legs, wipes the sweat off his brow, and finds staring back at him a woman, somewhat frumpy and very cute. It is his childhood sweetheart. They are overjoyed at the reunion. Bubba walks through the carriage into another one. Vasi still wanders

.   The train stops; there is some movement of people embarking and disembarking. Zeigler enters whistling through nicotine stained teeth, a cap worn precariously over his greasy hair looks as though it could fall off but it is pinned down. He carries a huge smoking pipe in his pocket. A stained cloth bag is hung on his shoulders. Almost instantly, he sees his parole officer in the carriage. He turns around and leaves the carriage with the Parole Officer (PO) becoming animated-agitated. The PO gets up but is blocked by Vasi still in search of a seat. Zeigler leaves the carriage and hides in the bathroom. The PO finally manages to leave the carriage but cannot find Zeigler. Vasi is about to go to the seat, but someone else takes it. Vasi returns to the previous carriage with Bobo and Marko.

In the meanwhile, the train stops and Zeigler gets out. The PO cuts a comic figure as, frustrated, he sees Zeigler make a laughing run for his freedom.

Back to Nico and Marko's carriage. Vasi enters. Bobo gets up to go to the toilet. Vasi deftly takes his seat. Bobo returns but Vasi pretends to be deaf. Bobo is again without a seat. He walks to the end of the carriage and finds another seat, sighs and sits down. He sits across from a young boy who tries to be friendly with him. Bobo smiles. In the meantime, a woman returns to sit beside the boy. Bobo is stunned; it is his wife who had run away with the child. They have a loud reunion. He is very affectionate with the child who is confused by the entire spectacle of the reunion.

A gypsy girl in all pink stands in the space between two carriages trying to jump rope in the rackety train. The door opens. Dimitri runs out shouting; he has a knife in his hand and is looking for Maria who hides behind some luggage with another man. Dimitri does not see them and runs into the next carriage.

The gypsy girl and her brother dance and sing about life being about changing places. Governments change, husbands change, wives change places. Even mothers and fathers change places. So where is my place? It is in my heart as the stars are in the sky, the gypsy girl sings....

The ticket collector rushes by in an attempt to catch Dimitri who stands like a mad man outside the carriage. The TC whistles to catch Dimitri's attention. Another man in uniform arrives; they hold down Dimitri who is not a big man. But po po po, Dimitri is the son of the railway chief. In a moment of triumph, they look at each other and decide simultaneously to "then pirazzi," so they tie his hands, pour ouzo down his throat, gag him and throw him into a small luggage space. The song continues.

The train stops. Our Bubba steps out and looks around him. Wipes crumbs off his face. From his pocket takes out some papers which fall out of his hands, and he struggles to disengage the papers from some thread that may have caught them in his pocket. They are a sheaf of tickets that he has been playing with—the tickets have deftly changed hands. Out also fall a pack of cards—all aces and but one Jack.

The song continues; the train leaves.

An older gypsy woman sees Bubba at the station and calls to her band of people who surround him wanting to know about him, wanting his goods, his money. From his pocket falls a button that rolls a few feet away and comes to a stop. It has on it the words: "Peace, man!"

So the story goes...Man entertains man; man leaves with a note of more-than-hope in his heart. It is common to experience such interludes on train journeys, if one is open and ready to be involved. Let comedy be our way through all our journeys.

We move on towards Katerina.

Soon we are in Katerina, where we meet our new driver, Vasillis, and new guide, Elpida, who will become a traveling companion. I request that we all get Greek names as we travel the land. She says she will think about it. I tell her when I had taken an African Literature class with Dr. Issa I had asked for a name. He'd suggested "Njeri," the wandering one—a *musafir* is wanderer or traveler of sorts. How apt that was for one who is always on journey.

In my French class, I had become "Anais". Now here in Greece, I am to find new names. Nothing will be lost, only expanded with new names, even for a short while.

We drive to Dion where we eat and visit the Dion site of the Macedonian kings. I tell Elpida that I just want to see Alexander, the thirty-year-young king, son of Phillip, who had traveled to India in 326 BC. She understands. When I tell her that I came here to liberate myself from myself, she laughs and says that is what her daughter says when she visits India. I've heard that one before, of course. People I have met say they visit India to lose themselves. I don't want to lose myself, just free myself, little realizing then that just proclaiming "I am free" is to be so and believing it. Taking responsibility for all I have lived is to make myself free.

I am free if I say, "I am free!" If I say, "I am not," then I can come with a hundred reasons to justify that claim. Why claim the latter? We are often intent on claiming what does not serve us. I am free! So it is. I start wondering at its meaning, then choose to go past the semantics and enjoy the ruins that lie sprawled decaying in time's endlessness. What really does it mean to be free?

Ruins lie layered in each of us and its information lies buried. Perhaps I look too much into things; perhaps, this is like the Renos Haralambidis' character in *No Budget Story* saying, "The soul of the Eskimo is an abyss." Okay, let's free the soul of the Eskimo so it does not sink into the abyss, like the abyss that is downtown in any big city, in any heart. Not the downtown that is a gay city, but the downtown worn out by filth, time, mold, urine in corners, rags, where the hungry wander in search of coins for a draught of forgetfulness. The abyss. It lives in each of us and rises in moments of despair or utter loss. Again polarities in our environments mock our existence. As we seek balance, I wonder if what we seek is clarity of neutrality. Perhaps, this is what we need in order to make sense of life situations, a place from which to make responsible decisions, a place from which to be responsibly free.

The day is warm, and sweaty smells pervade the air along with a heavy moodiness. Members of the group are becoming fidgety with the rushed schedule. We are being tested. Our limits are put to the test. After some mishaps on Kea with sweet and sparkly Jolie and pensive Nina hurting their feet, with Jolie losing and then finding her wallet, we have been on a relatively fine onward movement. A lot more is to happen. Seamus, the facilitator, reminds us we are to

Chapter 6 ~ Friezes in the Sun...
Discoveries

On June 20, we are ready for a tour of both Pella and Vergina, originally land of the Macedonian kings. The capital of Macedonia, Pella was found by King Archelaus; it later became the center for both Phillip II and his son, Alexander. Later, the center of the Macedonian kings was taken over by the Romans, who took the treasury back to Rome.

There are variations on the etymology of the word "Pella." One suggestion is that the word meant "a ceremonial place where decisions are made"; another that the word suggests "stone" or a "powerful defense on a cliff." That several Greek cities bear names similar in sound points to the last as a likely meaning. Somehow, decisions are made in ceremonial places; some might lead to foundations solid as rock hence providing powerful defense. Variations in meaning arise through sociological interpretations of ancient languages that sometimes create something new: it is suggested that the word "*polis*" emerges from "*pella.*"

What of its dual meaning of rocky foundations?

The center lies sprawled under the hot summer sky; its pebble mosaic lies naked to our wandering eyes. Despite its precision and beauty, we hear some tired feet trudging around in bouts of enthusiasm. It is noteworthy that Greek poet Timotheus of Miletus composed some of his verses here. Renowned Athenian playwright Euripides wrote amid these walls his *Bacchae,* a play about the arrival of Dionysus whose ways sought to liberate a largely conservative lifestyle and kingship in a structured society; the play debuted here in about 408 BC (sweet synchronicity with my room number).

We learn that young Prince Alexander was tutored here by none other than the great Aristotle.

Historic images and tales lie woven in the dust of memory. We hearken to it and move on taking bites of knowing to the next place—and to the next as though we walk in and out of dreams.

We leave the vastness of Pella of antiquity and move on to Vergina and are stupefied by its magnificence. In Vergina is an underground monument to Phillip II, father of the short blonde Alexander the Great, who set out to conquer the world, beginning with Persia in revenge for its invasions of Greece.

Vergina is a highly sophisticated monument to the majesty of these kings. The tomb has been excavated and a museum built over it, so people enter here and then proceed to the underground. Architecturally, the tomb is fascinating, so deftly designed that no one can enter without access to the doors, which are locked from the inside, seemingly with no other way out. The keying system is unique and complex, so someone important must have the secret to this treasure of the Macedonian kings.

Opened to the public in the late 1990s, this site displays a marble sarcophagus, Doric friezes, and paintings among various other objects. Most notable, of course, in the museum is the Vergina sun, a symbol used by the Macedonian kings. Also known as the Argead Star, this sun has sixteen rays; it seems to have belonged to Phillip II of Macedon, though there has been dispute about its original user.

The power of symbols extends beyond time and place. Greece, Cyprus, and the Republic of Macedonia have claimed this brilliant sun. The Native Americans also have such a symbol woven in their blankets. Indeed, it is a universal symbol of power and regeneration. Are we all Sun seed? Or Moon seed? Who are the *Suryavanshi* whose stories are told in the Indian epic, the *Ramayana*? The word *"Suryavanshi"* suggests race or Dynasty of the Sun or Solar Dynasty. We all must have common origins. We do.

Where did we begin our journeys?

On our walk back to the bus, I see trash strewn around and wonder what future archeologists would say about our contemporary civilizations—not its pottery but about its plastics and man-made fibers, about its mega-destructive capabilities, about its excessive domination over nature from the materials created for industry and manufactured in mass quantities, about its isolation revealed from the design of cities, about the extent of its libraries and information systems from all the motherboards in the rubble, about the temples of art—both good and bad—from all the museums. What would they say about the chair-like toilets of the Wild West?

I have now seen portraits of the great Alexander, the man with the slightly turned stiff neck, and my curiosity is sated. He seems to have come from strong familial roots, this man who listened to his horse, Bucephalus, who, once they reached Bafle-e-Az in Kashmir, India, turned around to face the direction of home. Alas, Alexander never made it home to Vergina. He died on the way back at about age thirty-three, having become known widely as a smart conqueror. His vision to conquer the west after having touched eastern lands was halted.

A town in current Pakistan carries the name of this famous horse, Bucephalus, who died following injuries in a battle. Legend has it that he was known for his good sense, and Alexander respected him for this. Horses are highly revered in ancient tales for their direct and deep instinctive connection with greater wisdom. Not only was a horse symbolic for its beauty and passion to Poseidon, the great god of the oceans, but also this inordinately beautiful being assisted in the expansion of lands. In Indian mythology, a horse was left to roam, and where he stopped was seen to be a sign to draw a new boundary marking expanded territory.

It is interesting to note how widely revered was the white horse in many lands. In India alone, Prince Siddhartha's favorite horse was Kanthaka, who died of a broken heart when the prince became the Buddha and left. *Ashwamedha*, a Vedic fertility ritual (or land expansion), involved a white horse for the sacrifice. Kalki, the tenth incarnation of Vishnu

107

not yet here, is envisioned to appear on a white horse. Similarly, Korean and Islamic cultures also mention a white horse, whose connection with lightning is interesting. Perhaps the white horse was a quick messenger of the light. The image of horse pulling the chariot of the Sun is also a popular motif.

Horses appear in legends and myths of many lands. The Norse god Odin has an eight-legged horse named Slepneir; how many directions did he cover? The Slavic war and fertility deity also used a horse for its prophetic ability; why do we have war and fertility in one god? Horse is also central to early Zoroastrians, to whom it represented the star Sirius. Such connections represent a complex cosmology, with which we seem to have lost touch in these high technology times, but whose symbols are distorted in shadowed sci-fi tales. Perhaps there was a time when humans and animals shared closer ties and communications.

I am compelled to note that horses also represent power and passion of sensuality and sexuality as we see in more recent times explored by English author D.H. Lawrence in his *Women in Love*. In these our current seasons, we know of horse whisperers who so acutely understand horses as to befriend them and remove all rules and programming of violent taming. Indeed, horses are now also masters of communication: they teach us how to ask for what we want; they teach us to know who we are. The eyes of a horse will strip you from your inauthentic behaviors and beliefs. Horse will insist on you being present and grounded. I speak from spending time with horses whose presence I love. This could be a book in itself.

Horses are beings of tremendous wisdom and mystical awareness. I say listen to the horse and let the horse lead you to your true self. Only then imagine traveling on Pegasus, the Greek horse of wisdom and of play.

Landscape of Epic and Poetry

We've spent the day in the ruins listening to stories of grandeur in narratives of kings, and we return to wonder about the blending of myth, landscape, and history. It is befitting that we segue in the evening to Theo Angelopoulos' world. He is a filmmaker whose work I have admired for many years. I am to meet him in Crete. I do not know yet this is in store for me.

In the evening, we watch part of his famous film, *Eternity and a Day* (1998). Its sweep is dramatic and poetic. Even though it does not follow typically the conventions of the epic genre, it is epic in its breadth—for the vast story underlying the rich narrative is interwoven with minute narratives like arias. My friendly colleague Seamus had noted that if I were to say these words to Angelopoulos he would appreciate it, for he wishes to leave us with films that are of epic proportions. These are interior epics, I say, for the story is of an aging poet whose one salvation is an encounter with an Albanian child whom he helps and from whom he learns of the transcendent power of words. I'd seen the film before. It is layered poetry.

I want to watch more of his films. I realize that in most video that I have shot in the last two weeks, I have used slow pan and zoom in and out. I, too, like to gradually enter and leave the subject. It is another way to create relationships with the characters, be they people or landscapes. It is another way to paint poetry—one with details that sweep the eyes and souls of the viewers, with words that emerge anyway, somehow, without warning because they must as part of a sweeping vision. I remember the gigantic hand that travels high in the sky in the opening shot of his *Ulysses*.

It is on our drive to Vergina that Elpida gives me the name "Ariadne." She says I remind her of Ariadne, one with pure soul. I protest that Ariadne was betrayed and that I don't want that association to continue with me. She says, "Okay, let me think." Did Dionysos' falling in love with Ariadne and marrying her shift the theme of betrayal? I do not know, but it feels better that the god of mad frenzy found her. I tell Elpida this; she says that is good because I look like Ariadne. She will show me in the national museum in Thessaloniki.

And then she gives me a look and says that because I bring her joy when she sees me that I am "Xara." I say okay.

She calls me "Xara" meaning Joy. In the museum, she looks for me, "Where is Xara?" as she shows us the finely carved bust of Alexander at Pella with a crooked neck. Here I am. It is an intense moment of destiny as I face him who invaded my land, he who conquered Taxila and its King Ambhi, whose nobility moved the youthful prince deeply.

The Vergina symbol of the sun is also displayed at this museum—were they also *suryavanshi,* the race of the sun, as our ancestors in our layered myths? Are we not cosmic dust—cosmic light that endlessly weaves the fabric in indefinable spaces?

Such rich diversities and mythologies must become mainstay of education again. Our students have no sense of these connections; we seem to be losing it as well. Such ignorance leads to violence.

Digressions on Way to City of the Sky

The next day we drive to Ouranopoulis, City of Sky or Heaven, to take the boat to and around Mt. Athos, home of many monasteries, and thus a place barred to women. Story has it that smooth-faced people would disturb the peace, so the hairy ones chose to stay sanctified in these beautiful awe-inspiring environs.

The drive to Halkidiki is beautiful. Seamus has us share with each other our story and what "journey" means to each of us. Why the clear waters here take me to my 1988 visit to Mexico I cannot explain other than perhaps I am reminded of challenges and absurdities through the land of the Maya and Aztec. Of course, my travels through Mexico also took me to homes of artists Frida Kahlo and Diego Rivera; to museums of David Alfaro Siqueiros and Jose Clemente Orozco, one of my favorite Mexican artists, whose painting of *Prometheus* hangs in the library of Pomona College in Pomona, California. My visit further took me to see the works of Rufino Tamayo, Fernando Ortega, the Iturbides and others.

I recall the old journey to many cities and to San Jeronimo near Zihuatanejo.

Not finding any accommodations in Zihuatanejo, my traveling companion and I slept on a beach bench. In the middle of the night, I awoke with a strange feeling to find someone slaphappy lost drunk sitting near me—the bench swarming with ants. Alarmed, I got up and found myself parched with thirst. This is how we met Jose, a twenty-six-year-old night watchman of the hotel across the street.

Assuring us all was okay, he took us to the hotel and gave us water. He found us a place to sleep in the restaurant and early the next day, invited us to his home for breakfast—said his mother would be delighted.

We arrived at a modest house with a big yard where his family lived. At the back were two separate suites: one for his sister and one for his family of wife and child. For some reason, he found it delightful to make fun of his "fat" wife, and then had his mother make us eggs laid by hens who clucked busily in their yard.

We relished the meal, listened to the news of the Cuahtemoc election, and when it was time for us to leave, he quietly requested that we get him some beer in exchange for marijuana. We politely declined and hurriedly made our way out to take the bus back to the city and continue the journey to Mexico City. That was it with Jose: breakfast, *cerveza*, and a "no thanks" to his offer of marijuana.

One journey recalls another and I take myself to my meeting with Margarida in Portugal at a film festival. She is a well-known writer of children's stories. After our meeting and conversation about energy medicine and a session that cleared her back of pain, she was intrigued and turned her attention to studying holistic medicine.

My ticket to Portugal was birthed in Huy, Belgium, which I had familiarly called the "southern part" of this little country. The Belgians had laughed at my reference to "South Belgium" because they said the country is so small that it's funny to hear of a north and south (politically, though, we know otherwise). It was at the short film festival in Huy that I'd met the director of the Algarve Film Festival. Here I'd won the Best Original Story Award. Here the Algarve Festival director had invited me to jury a short film festival in Portugal.

I had fallen for it and loved my time there reviewing short films.

I learned that it is not just that we are in search of stories, for they abound in us, but that stories are in search of us who are the tellers and makers. With this thought, I return to my traveling companions on the bus to Halkidiki.

Yes, I am in Greece on a tour with other writers from a little-known writer's program, and I reflect on my Greek connections in LA. Though I have been to Greek parties, danced the Sirtaki, and seen Damos (an Angeleno) break dinner plates, being in Greece far surpasses these episodes. I feel a deep mythic connection with Greece, more here in Saloniki than in Athens. I muse at the manners in England, Germany, and Austria; style of expression and hospitality vary in colder climates. People in Germanic lands express themselves with reserve, while here folks are more "ekphrastic" with what seems to be a hint of reserve. We are layered landscapes, made unique by cultural norms and taste of foods, but deep inside our psyche, we know archetypes make us cousins. Traveling to foreign lands moves us to our heartbeat, reminds us of our greater selves—a lack of such connecting triggers images of far distances, and this feels harshly alienating. While alienating moments are aplenty, there are those who remind that we belong to their land.

Once we reach Halkidiki, we have some moments of tension. Do we keep the driver and the bus while we take a boat ride, or do we let him leave for a bit? He has a burst of heat reaction and becomes vehement about time. Says that if we are not back from the boat ride by a specific time, he will leave us here and we would have to find our way back to Saloniki.

We walk through a mélange of restaurants and finally decide to split up to eat; we each desire a different repast. The food is same, yet different. No beer for me even in this heat. We rush through our meals so as not to miss the boat ride.

The crowded boat pulls away from the harbor after we have all happily pushed our way to the edges to look at the waves. I walk around to experience all the views and run into a joyful Doros dancing on the boat, which continues its weave in the waves around Mt. Athos. Doros is from Crete. All excited and laughing, she says I look as though I am from Crete. The odd thing is that I've been told again and again that I look Cretan, yet none of these people I meet who are from Crete look anything like me. They are all about a foot shorter than me, all on the fatter side, and have more rounded features. So I wonder who the other Cretans are whom I am supposed to resemble. I am curious. I am yet to see Ariadne's statue. Elpida, our guide, has promised to show it to me.

Doros and I communicate in two languages. Clearly, she is enjoying the freedom of being on the boat as she preens among us from the US. She takes off her blouse to bare herself to the winds and the sun. She looks at me and laughs as though to explain a tiny glimmer of guilt-at-pleasure joy. I reassure her it's terrific to be naked among the elements. It is as the gods would have it so we can be in our innocence. She laughs and insists that I must call her when I am in Crete. Later she gives me her phone number. I wonder how we will communicate on the phone when we cannot see each other's eyes and gestures. She insists; I smile.

I run into Doros in the shops after the boat ride; she insists she will be waiting for me in Crete. I say okay. Elpida amusedly translates for us. Soon, Doros and I part company as the boat veers its way toward land. What part of my destiny lies in Crete, I muse, on that island rich with nature's wonders, mythical places and the gorge? But for now I must be content and enjoy what unfolds.

After the boat ride, we wander away into restaurants and miss the designated hour by five minutes. That is enough botheration for Vasillis who decides to drive away and come for us an hour later. This means we miss seeing the other village where some of us were going to swim. *Then pirazzi!* Again, I run into Elpida at a shop that sells beautiful icons. The one I want to buy costs three hundred euros. The woman at the shop lets me take pictures of it while commenting on my eyes. She says she can see into my soul. I say people see themselves in each other—I do not say why what they see can shake them up sometimes, if what they see triggers them somehow. Tzimis in Athens had said that I know how to push the "red buttons" when I asked if he wanted a picture of a gorilla. He's a funny man, this Tzimis, knows a lot about herbs but not so much about how to soften the heart. He's abrupt and cannot, must not be crossed. He also said never to mention him in my story. People are irresistible; Tzimis with his bursts of wise sayings can be charming. Will he ever read this story?

The wild and raving heat god, Helios is magnanimous in great proportions. It's stupendously hot in this little village of Ouranopoulis. I long for the cool hotel room and the openness of Thessaloniki, which I have come to like. It is more expansive than Athens, which I remember to be very busy and contracting—one of the worst urban sprawls that I have visited. We start our drive back to Thessa. Seamus plays the last half of *Eternity and a Day* (1998) for us; I fall asleep. The wind and the water have either sated me or left me drained, not sure which. I desire the comfort of a plush sofa in a gentle nurturing space: a gentle grounding burgundy sofa in a hint of peach colored room, something like home, where the light is gentle and the music soothing blue.

Back in Thessaloniki, we freshen up for a bit, then take a long walk down the neighborhood to the home of Annike and her husband, Stefanos, both filmmakers who run a visual arts school for children. Stefanos shows us a clip of his film. He is proud of it. But the crude sex scene lacks decorum; some of us cringe. He persists with strange lack of grace, defends his perception and creative design, which many of us find degrading to both men and women—this insistence on his own "genius" seems to be his characteristic style of operation. I wonder how he gets away with this. The scene does not contribute to story or character development. What theme or conflict it highlights for us cannot be known. Besides, the male protagonist smokes relentlessly with no sense of making love; it is simply a non-sensual sex act. I find him puffed up, uninteresting. Stefanos will not be pleased with my utter disdain of his vision, craft and story, were he to ever find these pages. I wonder if the character is the filmmaker...!

The next time we meet in a cafeteria, Stefanos is not pleased. Annike, I say, should be on camera. She should have played Medea in their production of the same story. Stefanos wanted "some gal." Well, he got some gal.

How the Gypsy Boys Sang

Walking back from the café-studio, I lag behind and lose the group. I make a wrong turn and come upon two young gypsies. They sing and cavort with me, my camera. I am reminded of Tony Gatlif's film, *Latcho Drom* (1994), which in a lyrical and beautiful way traces the travel of the gypsies from India to Spain. The loud plaintive song sung by the ten-year-old Indian boy in the beginning sounds much like the song of the ten-year-old boy in Spain. Now, here are two young ones running around me. They are playful, wild, crazy storytellers.

I take a risk by talking with them. I gesticulate that I'd film them. So they sing for me; I record them. But they want to hold my camera; I won't let them. When I see two or three older guys arrive, I know it is time to zip my bag and prepare to leave. I wish I had more time with these two young boys, free and wanton in their ways, maybe also wanting in their ways, always on the go.

I sense them looking in my direction. Their look is somewhat invasive, not comforting. Their innermost thoughts remain hidden, but for their glances of wildness and propriety and, feeling beaded with panic, I leave them. But I have lovely moments on my camera and walk down the street. I look back and see the young ones being roughed up by the older boys.

Such moments occur frequently in large crowded cities. I wonder about the life of vagrants. How do they survive? What is freedom? Is it freedom to have to search for food and be denied land everywhere you go? Many gypsies, or Roma, have been landless and homeless wanderers; they steal to make ends meet, they dance wildly to celebrate, they are brutal when they have to be, claiming their brethren in ownership. At the same time, many Roma are well settled in "regular" work and live like "ordinary" people do, people like us. While filmmaker Tony Gatlif tells the stories of the Roma with a poignant eye, capturing their dances, music, and travails, he also shows us how some Roma are seen to be a "nuisance" to folk passing by. It is not uncommon for travelers to be robbed in trains, parks, and buses by young and adult gypsy boys and girls. So we must be aware. But we know thievery abounds in well-suited booted folk in high-rise offices.

Everyone must eat. For some people, just eating a meal means freedom. Stealing a loaf of bread as in Victor Hugo's *Les Miserables* is an act of survival—since stealing is wrong, how can a system be designed so everyone can afford to feed their families? An episode in this same famous book explores an unusual act of kindness on the part of the Bishop from whom Jean Valjean steals a pair of silver candlesticks. When police bring Jean back, the Bishop notes he had gifted them to Jean. This act reveals a kind side of the Bishop and this transforms Jean.

Here might be the "other" freedom, the freedom to choose how to respond to each singular moment. Biases arise in many ways. Certainly, we are affected by religion and culture, which govern our choices and our freedom to be. Are we free in essence in the state and quality of our inner being as the Bishop reflects? How might we nurture our relationship with our self and, in doing so, be free?

In such interactions, we meet the "other" in ourselves, we find new mirrors triggered in us, we learn a new song with notes that may be strange because they are new. If we cross boundaries in our attempt at relating, do we lose touch with the horizon? Or do we come in closer touch with our hearts— a new horizon? One that keeps eluding our grasp even as we feel a little bite or taste of it.

Listen! My heart sings
of antiquities where were birthed
horizons of light

May old songs awaken
splintered hearts of nations
so we long for home

Eyes hungry like night
dance to belong like stars: an
unending embrace...

Listen to me...just listen
Do your hearts hum
in unison like night?

Will you run in filthy rags
laugh like wild wind while stealing
a morsel of bread

or wear armani
pull the plug on guileless folk
who drink your lies unto the end?

The playful endearing eyes of these Roma boys with dark wavy hair seduce me into questioning my life. The choices I made or were made for me under the shadow of culture. Why I feel I must be in a hurry to get things done, so I lose the value of deeper relating. I run even when I am still. So I remain in longing.

Longing has a beauty of its own, but to be fulfilled is glad wonderment. How must I stop running and making excuses that keep me away from what I truly desire? Twinkles lift as I watch these boys play and sing. I can only imagine what might happen to them when they are scurried away by the older boys, who would school them into the ways of the Roma.

They know no other way.

way of wanderer ... take what comes
she rubs her toes in dry dust

from corner of her eye watches
a wing in the sky...
how it lifts the sunlight

117

"The gods, likening themselves to all kinds of strangers, go in various disguises from city to city, observing the wrongdoing and the righteousness of men."

~ Homer

other incarnations appear in various cultures. The sacred aspect of the bull is clearly known in the Indic world, even in the pre-Aryan Indus Valley Civilization IVC in India. Pashupati, Shiva with his bull or Lord of the animal world, is said to have originated in the Mohenjodaro and Harappa cultures. Shiva with his bull, a powerful image in India, is worshipped today with zealous devotion.

Shiva and Shakti are noted to be pre-Aryan; could making the bull Shiva's *vahan* be a later perhaps Indo-European adjustment? Making the bull Shiva's *vahan* suggests that the syncretism between the two periods—the IVC and the Vedic—was complete. Shiva is an emergence or evolution of Pashupati of the IVC, with the bull adopted into his entourage. We call this great bull "Nandi." *Vahan* simply means vehicle and represents the great god to whom he is attached.

Continuing the theme of Cretan origins, Aeolus also suggested that the Dravids of the Pre-Aryan Dravidian civilization, which flourished in Southern India, "are the same" as the Celtic Druids. He bases this on similarities between the words "Dravid" and "Druid" suggesting also that the word "vid" (knowledge, the act of seeing) gives us the word "video." He posits that those peoples are people of wisdom, of knowing. He notes that this linguistic comparison suggests a Celtic connection with the Indo-Aryans, which may not be so far-fetched as we see in linguistic records and mythic symbols.

It might be a stretch to say that "we all come from the same place," but Aeolus insists on it. Can Aeolus' insistence that we all come from Crete have some truth to it? Maybe, this suggests an Indo-Greek connection of a pre-Aryan time? Could these similarities not be a result of nomadic wanderers spilling cultural seeds and transmitting memetic codes? Or were there some other unknown or unrealized miscegenation source codes? Musings invite me to ponder on these possibilities.

It does not matter to me who came first but where we are going with what we know. This matters.

Perhaps, people paid more attention to the meandering constellations, which have powered communities and influenced their memetic codes. Arising narrative structures show us common origins and overlapping storylines in spite of great distances and only seemingly unrelated language groups. Today, shifting national boundaries and separations are urging people to re-discover one-ness of source and manifestations and to learn that we, indeed, are sound-light frequencies!

New stories are emerging. I wish to claim our mutual origins and participation in creating anew so all sentient beings discover and recognize wholeness as a series of unities.

I grew up with stories of Shiva and Shakti who together illustrate a primordial balance in the universe—masculine-feminine principles in a divine dance. So do Krishna and Radha, whose love is surely marriage of divine cosmic beings. Among the Greek gods, stories of primordial creativity reveal birthing in a sort of violence—Kronos swallows his kids, Europa gives birth to Europe following her rape by a bull, and Leda is raped by Zeus, who appears in the guise of a great white swan.

But these might be events in the skies. Cosmic disturbances are violent. Such stories of anthropomorphic gods explain creation of lands and shifts in constellations.

Reincarnation and study of moral life have usually been the purview of religionists and philosophers. Many Greek gods running rampant in the universe indulged in promiscuous acts, while they also ruled with supernatural magical powers. Perhaps it was all a morality play gone awry, or fertility rites taken over by the wrong lords, for even though these lords must have visited the priestesses of Delphi, the center—*omphalos* of the ancient world—whose Oracles were always cryptic, the men must have chosen wrongly. It was never for the Oracle to choose for people. The priestess always offered two answers.

The choice was always left to the person who raised the question. Ultimately, the message reminds: *Gnōthi Sauton*, "Know Thyself!" And it so is. So it shall be.

Here is the journey; what do you choose? Will you find your source codes? What is your single most precious virtue?

The fall of Minoa ended this power as well as the moral structure. Such power in the hands of women must make men mad with envy. Herein is one tragedy of modern man, suppressing what was earlier the purview of woman—learning and being keepers of the sacred—and denigrating woman in favor of structures now impoverished of spirit. May Mnemosyne stir in us memory of the right forms of creative imagination, so we may dream into action worlds that enrich and enliven, which bring us back to creating with right choices that nourish our relationship with nature and the cosmos.

The study of morality and power structure is a study of our behaviors in mythological tales, archetypes, and in our politics. The new mythology corrupted the feminine worldview, sourced her wisdom, misappropriated women's rituals, and established a system that encouraged the best and the worst of human sensibility. It is saddening to see a roughness and carnality in social behaviors, and I wonder how much here in Greece was influenced by the corruption of early stories. People seem dissipated, worn out. Of course, there are other factors also.

And this is true of people in many lands: the fatigue of living is a result of our divorce from nature, this separation the result of a rigidly coded urban lifestyle, part economic strife, and even an indulgent self-centeredness. I feel disturbed by this, for this state of being worn out is a result of losses, grief, stature, livelihood, extreme competition, and loss of innocence, of healthy playful childlikeness. The result is a lack of masculinity at its refined apex and femininity in her fullness. As ecological beings, we all suffer.

Violation on all levels leads to civilizations self-destructing. Could this then be another reason for the fall of the Greek civilization in the winter of all our discontent? Perhaps, the Romans who appropriated Greek gods by giving them new names were better organized, took over with a fresh vitality, and were skilled conquerors. Now we see what is happening with the hubristic US empire falling, falling ...!

Hunger for power creates distortions.

Whatever the reasons, my evening with eager storyteller, Stavros, is replete with tales and possibilities. He asserts storytelling enriches one's self-definition; sometimes, he sounds like an intrepid quasi Oracle of Civilizations...!

Love the Labyrinth:

Step into the labyrinth – find there your naked self. Watch how you stand, sit, eat. Watch your every move. Watch what the trees say. Listen to the trees. Watch how the animals arrive and threaten your every stance. Watch how you lift your feet. Watch your desires unwind your structures. Watch your eyes darting in fear.

Watch your hunger: you are the hunger of the world.

You will ache for the gold. You will ache for serenity. You will hunt for beauty and find the void. When you come into this dark empty space that never ends, you will find not a bag of gold, not a bag of ambrosia, not this...you will find nothing.

Be you content with this nothing and not with conquest, not with political power, not with usurping the world's resources, not with destruction of self and others... Be you joyful at this fullness, then you would have arrived.

Then I will protect you for you are that—that which I am waiting for. Love the labyrinth: it is the temple of your body, psyche, soul, anima.

You are the labyrinth you travel to make whole. Look up in the hungry night sky: There am I! Containing you! Showering you with dewdrops in the dawn light.

Watch how you listen! Open your heart!

124

An Evening with Stavros

I shall fast-forward here and return later, for the story with the Athenian Stavros belongs in this place. We have met in Athens through a mutual connection. He has invited me and two other associates to his place for a meal. Stavros, so full of meaning and symbolic interpretations, loves to share stories and reveal the new information and interpretations of mythological tales whose religiosity has remained buried under the cloak and yoke of Christian Orthodoxy.

My evening with Stavros, a surgeon happy with his life, is enriched with layers of meanings of words and names—I feel edified. We both love the story of Medea, whose name, he says, suggests the meaning "that which one must not do." So her killing her children only goes to show that she destroyed matter as a lesson to Iason for destroying the sanctity of the spirit, the soul. He can have or make babies anywhere any number of times, but his soul suffers as he acts without the understanding of greatness of the connection between spirit and matter. He acts only with regard to matter. That, itself, is wrong. For spirit is important. So this suggests again the woman revealing her knowing of that which was/is right, in order to keep balance in the universe—even though her act is deemed heinous. This must not be seen literally, but metaphorically. Stavros is clear on this.

There is a budding New Age movement in Greece, whose proponents have taken to yoga and meditation, to self-help workshops and ancient rituals of the east. In Los Angeles, people lead workshops in the Eleusinian mysteries, as people desire to understand more deeply their feminine self, which the US, a young culture *sans* ancient ritual and mythology, is hungry to explore. The *animus* is out of proportion and the *anima* is deeply bruised, which leads to injury of both, the masculine and feminine principles—our roles and functions to create a healthy society are in question. Being injured and wounded, both must heal to co-habit harmoniously, not live in perpetual struggle to control and be controlled—both must continually co-evolve and transform each other to keep us perpetually in love, in *agape* and *eros*. The universe is *eros*, for

125

it breathes and engenders. Both *agape* and *eros* create a weave together—a paean like the Krishna-Radha divine love, where both are container and essence, who together alchemize and potentize essence of each other.

Stavros explains that mythological stories show us the need to understand and to live with the demands of the spirit as well, to make the connection with matter for it is a continuum. Hence moral way is better but not if rigidified to *rigor mortis*. What has Greece done unto itself that men adopted ways of the anthropomorphic gods and lost the philosophy of the men and women who brought morality into the public sphere? How is a civilization broken, destroyed and de-spirited? When can it be re-built: matter woven with spirit—to make *eu-topos* instead of a *u-topos*?

I ask for meaning of "Ariadne."

"Ariadne," Stavros says, "means pure or purity." Her role in the journey of Theseus was to show him how to not remain stuck in the labyrinth (of life) with the Minotaur (the flesh) but to find a way out and purify the self. He found a way out of the labyrinth with the thread that Ariadne gave him (the *sutra,* the sacred thread), but he betrayed her. His karmic effect was to suffer the death of his father who waited looking for a boat with a white sail; instead, Theseus forgot and left the black sail on the boat. The father, thinking that Theseus was dead, committed suicide.

Ah, if Elpida the guide sees an Ariadne in me, what must I learn from my Self in light of the new meaning? Reflecting on my relationships brings home this aside— wanting so much to see purity in every one, I pulled wool over my own eyes. I hoped to see potential come to fruition and bear flowers. One cannot have an enriching relationship merely with idealizing of potential, for there is no growth or transformation, no mature masculinity (or femininity). Without lovingness the relationship is not a desirable one: in such a connection both are triggered to their smallness, not their bigness. Holding on when a partner has no will to grow can only bring loss, tears, and ache of heart.

Sad-delighted, I have moved away into greater spirits with myself for having traversed the labyrinth, for having

126

been guided by the *sutra* into a cave and out through a window to the light. Light keeps you alone, which bring its own dark.

> *Light, little sister,*
> *keeps one wanting,*
> *caves become walls...*

We are reflections of our myths. These inform us of our foibles and make us witness to potential of our own greatness. Nothing is immoral in the vast fabric of the universe: if the medicine has been endured. One ill-timed or wrong deed leads to blindness leads to suffering, which can result in the end of morality in a life. But to suffer is to journey; it must, then, have a destination. It must lead to illumination, or its purpose is denied in a life. How else is a life well lived?

I have gone ahead of myself and must return as in the oral tradition to an earlier time before my meeting with Stavros.

The thread of the narrative is not lost. Sometimes it winds in and out to places we are to discover, taking us to little dark pools, where dance sweet fools. They make me wonder where I am going with everything, even with this.

Light transforms everything. In light everything disappears. In the dark mischief happens. Everything also disappears. Better to disappear than to make bad seed. Bad seed makes bad deed.

Holy Day of Holy Days

The last days of the seminar are in Athens. As I dress for our flight to this august capital, I keep my dark blue hat to wear upon landing. It does not make its way out of the tiny plane and short flight from Saloniki. Things seem to be getting lost—I have a strange presentiment that something is afoot.

Embracing the heat, we are driven to the Hotel Plaka. I have a nice room here but wish for quiet days of rejuvenation.

127

Monday June 24th is, like so many other days, another Holy Day. We go to the Akropolis. What a treat to be in the midst of a dance of lovely ideas and proportions. The outermost pillars are wider in girth than the inner ones because mathematically they measure the same since the light that hits them makes them seem slimmer and thus equal to the inner columns. These columns also slant slightly in towards a center and, if built further above, they'd make a pyramid. Clearly this structure suggests the element "fire," ascending consciousness, fire of clarity—spiritual fire. The word "pyramid" suggests middle of fire, the ascending line.

Then the floor, which curves ever so slightly to create the illusion of straightness—when one views it from a distance, the floor looks straight. Such care and attention to geometry and stylized proportions with the metaphysical elements in mind are edifying. Great architecture always delights. Then the cityscape from these heights takes on a different tone. Imagine living in a place like this with a few homes spread at your feet for miles amid olive trees and fields.

In spite of all this knowledge from thousands of years of magnificent structures the world over, men have made horrendous cities in the last hundred years or so. Athens also offers examples of urban sprawls with some unholy buildings cramped around busy streets—this, too, around a powerful energy vortex. Too many people everywhere influence the etheric into which they have built inhuman structures; in such crowds, we do not always think our own thoughts further adding to confusion.

Crime abounds here in this energy vortex crisscrossed with uncertain intentions. Unfolding events reveal that it has become my destiny to be caught in the middle of the arms of petty criminals.

The Underworld

There is a vortex in this ancient city; people speak of it. They say the Akropolis was built on this powerful vortex. Does this vortex make people go mad? Greece is falling in so

128

many ways. Its finances are in the doldrums. Petty crime in the big city is a symptom of its denial to nurture an environment and means for the unfolding of humanitarian ways to sustain communities with employment, education, health facilities and enriching relationships. Yes, tourists come and enjoy the food, the antiquities, and local folk take pride in their history. But the underbelly of the city contains a network of locals and immigrants from nearby lands whose actions are not savory.

On our first morning here, we are scheduled to visit the Museum after the Akropolis. Taking the metro from Akropoli to Omonia was just fine. Then from Omonia to Biktoria, I become the target of thieves. Careful planning and group dynamic of the men who robbed me open my eyes to sleight of hand and to cunning body positioning and coordination.

The Metro is crowded and I am not able to move; rather, these guys block my every attempt to move leaving me feeling suffocated. Only after we get out of the train do I realize what has happened. This after Sean, a strong and observant writer in our group, jokingly asks, "So how many wallets did you all lose?"

This day turns out to be memorably historic: an adventure with the underworld, not Hades, but an interaction with real gypsies, sharp-eyed tramps, or very clever thieves. It is one stop from Akropolis to Biktoria on the Metro when these well-organized vagrants surrounded me and would not let me move. I did not feel them unzip my fanny pack. Zilch. I felt nothing except the need to move away from them. And couldn't.

This run-in with the thieves dominates the rest of my day. I am all wrapped in my confusion; I feel devastated, vulnerable, violated. Leaving the group, I take a taxi back to the house near Metamorfoseos. Thaleia calls banks for the phone numbers that I must call to report this theft. This Holy Day is like no other, and local contacts are closed. Godliness and crime work hand in hand. Naturally! We know religious institutions extract from the vulnerable for the sake of salvation, and criminals, too, have gods to invoke.

God-Mother loves everyone; we all are god's children.

By the time I am able to get through to the credit card companies, these boys have claimed stolen goods. Milos drives me to Beikou Police Station, but we are unsuccessful. We go to Omonia; the police send us on our way. We return to the house to speak with Thaleia, and then go back to Hotel Plaka. That night I do not sleep well. I am busy making phone calls and feel too tense to rest. Luckily, I am able to cancel the cards, and I know that I won't be responsible for the damages. So good to be with some American companies whose representatives commiserate so long that the phone card runs out of minutes. I have already lost five new phone cards in my wallet, four credit cards, and all other identification. Then I become wise and learn to call collect through AT&T.

All I keep re-seeing in my mind is responding to Sean with, "How can you lose more than one wallet?" then looking down to find my fanny pack open and my wallet gone. Then the restless night feeling alone and scared, knowing too well that I'd have to take care of it by myself and that I would. There was no point in fretting. So I became calm. I had learned well to say, "*then pirazzi.*" This drives me through the unsettling process. I laugh. Sometimes, laughing does not feel real, but it sees me through a rough patch.

The next day Athanas accompanies me to the US Embassy and the Omonia police station to report the theft. Thinking Athanas would be at work, I had asked for young Milos, cousin and friend of the family, to accompany me, but Athanas comes himself, noting that the boy "is not man" enough to handle the police. Greek manly ideals are imaged in the representation of a Hercules. Athanas is right. I feel amused.

Surely some good shall prevail. Life meanders in undulations.

My "Androgyne"

We have another delightful meeting with Renos Haralambidis, an engaging artist with a candid display of wit and silly humor. I feel entertained on this momentous Monday, the day the thieves won. It is evening and Seamus shows my short film, *Androgyne*; I still feel numb as if I am in another world.

It is horribly hot in the room, which has no fan or air-conditioning. So that is a problem, especially since the story is serious, demanding attention. The story is about a sculptor preparing for a show. But feeling her work to be ordinary, she is pushed to making a masterpiece, which magically comes alive and demands to be made human. But only one may be human: the sculptor or the sculpture. There is a tussle between maker and sculpture named "Androgyne", and the sculptor prevails, imbuing her art with the power to inspire people "to see what they need to, so they can grow and learn about love." So the sculpture slowly freezes in a new position to represent herself in her element: strength and grace. She is named "Androgyne" as she embodies qualities that make her, as she says, "a balance of opposites."

The serious nature of the story of my short film, the heat and fatigue, send a few into slumber. I am comforted by the responses of those that are awake. Leslie and Ellen tell me they appreciate the story and realize how much work went into its making. Annie loves it. Ricky tells me the flashbacks work. Seamus says it is impressive, and I agree with him that it could do with some trimming. He now realizes that I am able to make abstractions work. This is affirming.

He is referring to other story ideas that I have discussed with him—the one about the *Story Makers*, my story set perhaps in Los Angeles. For this I must watch *The Player* (1992) and another whose title I cannot recall in the midst of flies and humid heat. Selma, Miriam's mother, is delighted at the depth of the film. I am comforted. I still have to deal with the case of my stolen wallet, credit cards, car wash points, Vidiots membership, driver's license, five unused phone cards bought to make international calls, and other items. Ah, *then pirazzi*. I want to call my friend in Los Angeles to see how he is, to tell him of this misadventure, but I let the feeling pass through me, unwilling finally to take action. So much has happened.

I am up most of the night, and by the morning, I have been able to call all the credit card companies and take care of the problem. The calls cost me only $3.36. All my money will be returned; I'll have to complete some paperwork when I am back on familiar soil. Luckily for me, my passport was in another pouch behind the many-splendored wallet, which is now possibly rotting in some drain or gutter.

In Search of Completion

The next day after our final meeting in the afternoon, we celebrate with dinner at a wonderful *taverna* in the Plaka. This is where I eat *dakos* for the first time—*dakos* is typical Cretan bread. Dark and hard, it is served with fresh crushed tomato. I like it, but smile wondering what most people would do with bread that is dry and hard if served at home by one's mother. Here we are invited to serve ourselves the Greek way—pitch a fork into any dish and eat to enjoy. I am reminded of Ethiopean restaurants in Los Angeles where it is traditional to feed each other across the table in a communion of friendship or romance of sorts.

After dinner and festivities, we walk back through the Plaka, not to meet each other again. Some walk on through the lost and losing pathways of the Plaka for their last look and last few swigs of local beer Mythos, or ice cream, and posters of old movies, and trinkets that color the cobbled paths of this mercantile center. The night looks strange, as though a sheet had spread in its layers and the shops suddenly alive with last moments of longing; it feels already so far away.

Travelers must go on their paths, each following a trajectory self-chosen or those set for them. We carry bits of each other with us. I have received an award, an acknowledgement really, from the group for being calm about the thievery, for holding my own. It was in a circle on the terrace of the hotel that we shared our creative outpourings to reach completion.

I will not forget Haralambidis, noting that his next film might be about a victim mentality. I did take it all in; I think he

132

was being sardonic about my adventure, which they all think was a run in with Albanian youth, not Greek. Funnily enough, I was so impressed with the Metro thieves, I imagine doing a documentary on their adroit skill, their niftiness. I even go back with Milos to those areas one hot-hot mid-day and look in gutters and trashcans. But the heat and the impossibility of finding a stray frayed California Driver's License melt that desire out of me.

I have many projects to make my time travel ... Oh where is my Muse? Come to me!

...the Metro jangles my memory and flashes of sepia images superimpose on each other in succession leading me to the ringleaders; there are so many... And the pimps, innocuous looking men-boys, seemingly going about their business have a secret coded language—they know whom to pick—the unwary tired traveler, intent on making the most of their hospitality; or the one lost in ruminations of buried time; or the giggling one caring less of her belongings.

Their silent dance crowds people into a space, people are pressed into being like a single sardine amid many anonymous clothed persons, concentrating on nothing at all, but waiting to move on when the Metro stops, to continue their truncated lives in a new location.

The train stops. Everyone disperses in different directions. In search of a history that is also compressed, like the lost self, between pages of unwritten books, destined to be buried forever...

Until future memory unearths, stirs the retelling of story in a new way. For a new life...before the travelers lose their longing and forget... forget why they chose to be born.

Let us not forget our collective human destiny: to build a foundation of virtues, to practice the art of becoming whole, to be creatively nourished if we are artists of life.

On Wednesday morning, I return to my room on the terrace at the home of my hosts. I have to rearrange myself for the remainder of my stay there. Admittedly, for the next six to seven days, I feel at wits' end with low spirits. Athanas insists I take his vitamins and DHEA so I can balance depleted hormones in my body.

There is so much of Athens to experience. Having studied some Greek literature and taught Sophocles for some semesters, I want to take in all I can of the diverse but broken columns of existence in modern Greece. But I am choosing to be content with what I can do with ease, for I have no desire to push myself to do everything any more. I desire to enjoy slowness and subtlety. Well! A visit to the theater is a must, even just once. The distance and my seeming loss of passion make the Epidauros seem an eternity away, and it is impossible to watch all the plays. No one in the family is keen to go to the theater, but young Milos expresses a desire to experience one play.

The following Sunday we go to the Herodio Atticus Theater. For both of us it's a first; for me, it's a fantastic treat to be in this ancient space where many a dramatic action has delighted and educated masses about the laws of the universe and our relationship with it. Milos would have preferred if the play had been in ancient Greek. But this dramatization of *Medea* is a Spanish translation directed by Greek filmmaker Mihalis Cacoyannis. *Medea* is a story that powerfully survives time as noted earlier. Remember Jules Dassin's film version of the myth told with a classic complex of situations, story within a story that highlighted the dark feminine aspect, which we know if disturbed turns to destruction. Kali, as time, devours all. She loves fiercely us with adoring gaze.

Here, I take moving images with my PD-150 until the attendants warn me they will confiscate my $3,500 image-capturing machine. I stop, but not before I get some really classic images. The stage far down below, the thousand sitting spaces encircling the stage, the great dome of night above: as above so below feels apt. We are all stars for a few moments facing through the drama our own vulnerabilities and longings: to be known, loved, desired, to be whole, to be never betrayed.

When we come to a head, we must empty to make space for the new. Our errant ways and jealousies should have no room in the true marriage of love, but only in the light of play may we understand simplicity and surrender.

Leaving the Herodio Atticus is also an experience. The play is over, and I feel unable to move. I simply wish to sit on the stone seats and experience the vastness surrounding me as well as the intense smallness of being in the darkened night. I sit in silence until the attendants insist we leave. We are only mildly jostled in the lessening crowd. I am again reminded of how tenuous relationships can be. Here. There. Everywhere. Recalling such moments does not feel good.

A restlessness in me hearkens to the ancient days when plays were performed one after another to keep people reminded of the laws of balance in relations between man and man, man and nature, man and the gods. A *katharsis* would propel the audience to feel projections of self in unhealthy situations, to self-reflect, to know the difference, to maintain the balance we so desire. We must soothe our conscience; we must grace our lives with gratitude's grace; we must accept that balance is not a stasis but a dynamic dance. To lose everything is certainly tragic. Worse it would be if we learned nothing from errors of our *hubris*.

Art has a purpose. If we do not learn from our arrogance, we might learn through art's filter.

The drama at the Herodio is but a rich taste of what follows. I am thrown into greater drama in the household coupled with disagreements between the master and mistress; I have no desire to be witness to this. The excitement of the last two weeks and the damper thrown on me take their toll leaving me unable to take action on my own. Yes, I seem to have given up a part of myself and feel disempowered with fatigue.

The moon is rich and full, and the Grecian summer unfriendly. I surrender.

Brief meetings with people in the house remind me to steer clear of people's quarrels. As onlooker, I am in the midst of it all; space is a cultural context. If you are part of the funeral and the mourning, then you are part of domestic squabbles. But I am loth to watch my host run around in unseemly underwear with his wife trying to make him see reason in a voice climbing the walls, perhaps to run away from the intent of the speakers. Imagine, rotund men running around in loosely hanging old cotton underwear and being autocratic at the same time. Get them to a laundry machine or to a nunnery, or a monastery, better yet to a sports center. Imagine a petulant sundry portly Caesar in a diaper and crown of victory strolling the Akropolis, waving to a crowd because a star shone only for him. Imagine!

I recall again I am part of the household.

I return to my room upstairs in the delirious heat. But seeing my listlessness, professor insists again I take more DHEA to raise androgen levels. It works; it lifts me out of my doldrums. I have more days here. I ought to be well.

In a couple of days, Thaleia takes me to a christening, and the same evening to attend a wedding. These cultural treats win me over!

A Christening and a Wedding

The christening, a beautiful rite of passage, is a richly layered ceremony. Highly ritualized, it is similar in some ways to our emotionally rich *naamkaran* (name assignation), the Indian naming ceremony. I listen to the priest chant in liturgical Greek as he holds the baby; the parents are excited and happy; the baby is formally given a name in the community and becomes a legitimate member. Relatives and friends all mill around, dressed in their finery despite the heat, fussing and congratulating the proud parents, aunts, uncles, and grandparents.

Everyone is dressed in wild finery; even for a few hours, it is customary to show off frills, fancies, fandangos, frocks with silk tassels, frumpy hats made to look tastefully

136

gaudy, faces with happy make up gone wild with perfumes and smiles. Oh yes, the dark glasses! Thaleia is also dressed in her fine jewels; her mother has been gone for a few weeks. Friends and acquaintances who have not seen Thaleia for some time commiserate over Galatea's death. After the official naming is done, we will all eat, then pick up little goodbye gifts before departing for the day.

The christening takes place outside a very small church. I enter the little old dark chapel; it smells old and well used with shadows, icons, memories, old notes of music. Wooded beams on the ceiling and wooden benches for pews suggest a rustic sacred space. I take pictures of this curious place, and when I leave I realize how welcoming people are—I was able to get in close and absorb the ritual in its richness, the singing and pouring of water and sacred chanting in Greek. I stand right by the parents and even the priest.

How wonderfully potent can a day be? I attend a christening in the morning, and in the evening, I witness a wedding with Thaleia, Athanas, and their associate. I meet the bride's father, who is so excited that he lets me in close to observe the ritual of marriage vows here, and, of course, I am ready with my camera. How many people would have such an opportunity on one visit!

At the onset, I am invited by the bride's father to stand close to the priest who is officiating. So I have a privileged position from where I can view most of the wedding. The bride is joyful in her long flowing bride's gown; the family and friends look appropriately attired; there is great festivity in the air. The priest reads vows; the bride and groom recite. Music rises to the high ceiling and out of the doors to the gently sinking night sky.

This church is a whole lot bigger than the little one of the christening. The grounds are also spread out; we can see the city from up here, lights twinkling to their own music. The night settles in beautifully. At a table together, my hosts, their friends and I enjoy a typical Greek meal of chicken, green beans, potatoes, and salad. Festivities fill the air with joy-sadness.

At the party after the wedding, I dance a bit, and sweetly, the bride comes up and holds my hands. We dance together. I am not so good at Greek dancing for I have taken just a few classes in Los Angeles. Grateful that the evening is a lot cooler than the baked morning, I become part of another cultural event. The joyousness of the community dance lingers in my toes. I wonder if I have ever been Greek in another life.

I am losing count of days and dates—the heat moves in and the night arrives, rolling in and canceling one day after another. Some days are more creative and calmer than others. I am biding my time so I can return. I wonder what more stories are in store for me here in Greece. I have yet to explore parts of Athens and to visit the islands. Am I being a glutton for living in moments of fantasy as Alice did in Wonderland?

I marvel that my visit to Greece began with a funeral, brought me to a christening, and then to a marriage. A letting go of parts of the self, followed by a rebirth, flows naturally to a *conjunctio*, a marriage an integration of self with Self. Somehow this flow begins to feel symbolic. Recalling that I had wanted my travels to liberate me from myself, I asked whether I had indeed been freed from myself. I had met with hidden selves and mirrors, been a mirror to others. I'd experienced variations of ecstatic moments, sadness, joy, curiosity, communion, frustration, hunger, indecision, joy of discovery, aloneness, wonder, insecurity, vulnerability, longing.

The next stage of the journey is revealing itself. I still have three weeks to learn more about the land and about myself. Yes. Always the drama is with our self. I have longed to have my own family, but the strange confinements of some have made me wary; naturally, I am convinced my way will be different from that of my parents' generation. Our sensibilities are different. The soothsayers that mother took on made a mess of things.

Some others insist my path is that of the spiritual seeker, whatever that means. Everything we do is part spirit anyway. Must we not balance all aspects that goad us into wholeness?

Being empty of myself is harder than thinking about it.

Void in me awakens
geometry of dance aches to smile
sun rises between my fingers

   light splinters sky
   ruins and fallen dust at my feet
   so many songs - a dithyramb

even dust sings
whose voice whispers over seas
longing gathers me whole

   tender is my soul
   I sing a tuneless note

   deep waters kiss my feet
   foam sinks into sand

      sing to me Muse
      of who I am – where is my home
      of union not bondage...?

   bring me to my singular unities
   and the world to its own
   by its own volition

      this is true power

"Nothing exists except atoms and empty space; everything else is opinion."

~ Democritus

Chapter 8 ~ Relationships That Reveal

Relationships—how we do this dance again and again. How we are born into it and die for it. How we learn through sorrows of loss and alone-ness. How expectations illumine shadows of our unfulfilled selves. How we fall and rise to learn that real loving is a discipline that enriches all our interconnections.

My time here has been touched by people who have taught me lessons, shown me their ways. Some sweet moments in Athens have been with Meropi, Polish Maria, and Milos. Meropi and I share a birthday. We are alike, yet so very different. Our social and educational backgrounds are poles apart. We have nothing in common at all. But we can smile together for a few moments. We share lessons of diverse life experiences. What is common is Mother Teresa as she was from Albania too. Polish Maria is always so very nurturing.

Milos is kind and earnest, but lacking in commitment. Unaware of what he wants, he is passive and bored like others in their twenties or thirties confused about life's purpose. Perhaps, in search, as we all are. He has made himself available to me if I wish to go somewhere. So one evening we visit his relatives, Selene and Lykaios. I take for them a pot of beautiful crotons, which I buy from a man at a flower shop near their home; it turns out this man has lived in Los Angeles, a city people love and hate.

We walk in Selene's garden and talk about her plants. She grows aloe, rosemary, and thyme. As I walk with Selene, I see she glows with an inner simplicity; she smiles fully and laughs joyfully. Lykaios seems content with his skill at carpentry; his garage is full of wood and broken tables that he might work on some day. Like an artist's studio, full of things being worked on if not physically, then in the mind somewhere. Milos seems to have inherited this quiet sensitivity from his parents; but his stubbornness keeps him from achieving goals.

On another evening, Milos and I visit the seaside in an area called Glyfada. I decide that I must swim. Unprepared for this, I dip in the waters again in my t-shirt and underclothes like I did in Karthea. It feels okay since other people on the beach are naked—it's the norm at this beach. He plies me with a towel and I dry off. After the swim, I lie covered with a towel and place rocks on my belly; this feeling of solidness brings me deep rest.

He is curious: why rocks on the belly? It feels very good I say. Restful.

We then go to a *kafé* where I eat *spanakopita*, my favorite spinach-feta pastry, and drink tea. We play knots and crosses and realize the gentle power of simple play without pressure. There is not the compulsion to be doing and accomplishing. When Milos drives me back home, he says we should have sat on the beach until 10 p.m. to enjoy the quiet of the evening. Maybe I say: quiet evenings by the water sound cooling and nourishing.

In a few days, Milos drives me to Piraeus so I can take the boat to Santorini. It is Saturday, July 6. I have to visit a bookstore on the way, so we make a mad dash for the market in the middle of the town. Driving to the big store, I tell him that everyone we meet is a ghost and that only he, Meropi, and I are real, that we talk to people to complete some old karmic stuff, and they are ghosts. He says maybe he believes me only a little; for the most part, he does not. At the bookstore, I run into Renos, the filmmaker, whose film we had watched in Kea. I buy a book on Crete; I feel I must buy Cavafy's poetry but can't find a copy. Strange the national poet does not lurk on a shelf at a store in the capital.

We walk back to the car. It is so hot that I have to buy more drinking water. Milos carries my camera bag for some time; it is a relief. When we pass a fountain, he says I could swim in there. He is referring to my dip in the sea some days

142

earlier. He assures me he is being mischievous, *piraktiri*: a new Greek word for me.

At Piraeus, we sit outside a nice quiet café. I drink tea and he drinks soda. Silence fills the space. Then I write him the Devanagari alphabet and show him how to write his name. He says it all looks very complicated and difficult. He writes me more Greek words; perhaps, I can use them on my trip to the islands. Then we leave for the boat. There is a bit of a run around to locate the boat I am to take. But he takes care of everything calmly; I feel grateful for I seem to be running in a state of nervousness. Could not have done it as easily without him—I tell him this as he makes sure to walk with me and carry my bags onto the boat. Small fleeting connections we make in our travels come to mean much in passing moments.

I am on my way to Santorini, a place of legend, lovers, and liturgy.

Settling on the boat, I find that my seat is too close to the smokers' seats, so I look for another one. My search leads me to a seat occupied by a bag between a Frenchman and a sleeping passenger. The bag on the seat belongs to the sleeping man, who wakes up and moves it. I have a new but smelly seat. Well. I read, I take notes, I eat, yes again, my *spanakopita*. It's easy to pack and take with me in case I don't find something delectable on the way. I buy some tea and have a sort of conversation with the Frenchman. He is impressed that I translate a small passage on the cover. I cannot speak French, but cognates are fun play. The man to my left is from Egypt. He studies in Athens. We reach Santorini at around 9:30 p.m.

Before we get there, I speak with another woman (Greek, married to an Italian) who simply just happens to know Popi from Kea. I make a mental note to tell Seamus this—he'd laugh at this synchronicity. Owner of the Hotel Karthea, daughter of Anna who had been very affectionate and caring with me, who had given me olive oil and cotton and bandage for my *athinous*-spiked big right toe. What chance in a million would there be of such a thing happening? I come from Los Angeles and visit Kea, where I meet Popi. On a trip to another Greek island, I run into someone who knows

143

Popi who turns out to be well known among the islanders. How we are related!

How stories do get around—the old traveling oral tradition. I am getting around: I am a product of an early system whose values and visions were transported first orally, then on paper—as this, too, is now recorded on paper, then electronically, to be reproduced on paper. Memories are continually being created.

Arriving in Santorini

Sometimes, we meet the same people twice, maybe even thrice. Each time they reveal parts of themselves carefully hidden in the folds of the psyche. If one is not careful, one can miss treasures and even demons of instruction.

When I arrive in Santorini, Iokaste, whom I had met on the boat from Kea back to mainland, is at the dock to receive me. Iokaste is daughter of Vara and had invited me to join them here. Her earlier warmth suddenly has a bite; her demeanor has changed; she is unlike her welcoming self back in Kea. I wonder what the matter is, for she had been so friendly before. We drive straight to where her party awaits. Vara lights up and is exactly as I remember her from back in Kea, as warm and joyful as ever. I remember how Vara had shared sweets with me in Kea. She laughs that I remember.

We visit an open-air bar and have a pleasant evening over drink and snacks. But what transpires later with Iokaste is not as pleasant as I'd wished to experience. My instinct had cautioned me loudly—why had I not listened?

Early morning blues hit us all; we share a suite with a very large drawing room, where I have a couch. Unable to sleep in the strange environment, especially with her father puttering around so early, I get ready to free up the bathroom for the stragglers—then step outside to take a walk and clip my nails. This irks Iokaste so badly that she lets me know her displeasure all day. If I had only listened to my gut instincts and not gone at all! It is too late for the "if only," and I am reminded of the lackluster aspect of remorse. Naturally, I

144

think Iokaste has been self-indulgent with her organized chaos of being a drama queen and not the most welcoming hostess—following her enthusiastic invitations to join the family, I feel I have been a naïve victim confused by her many faces ... and the shadow of my inability to say, "No." What darkness lurks in her psyche? Or mine?

Dreadfully the day unfolds, both day and I hiding from her anger and goaded by it. I wonder at her spiteful ministrations during the day, how driven she is by envy that she has already distanced her parents from me. What moves someone to be queen of mean? What karmic triggers have her wound up so? I have no answers but to make my getaway soon. To think how her mother doted on me in Karthea and on the boat! But given that my stuff is in their suite and I am a "guest," I am for some time in their hands—future plans will unfold in a few hours.

We spend the day touring Nea Kameni where we each go our way. My camera is my friend, so I take some fine pictures, epic images reminiscent of Bergman, touch of Angelopoulos, and even of Herzog, stark, symbolic, excessive expressions of man's desolation and indulgence in it. I see this in the rocks, the torrid heat, the crowds of tourists all in search of something to make them happy; sometimes, all this feels like a strange ritual, going through the motions of making things happen so there are stories to tell. Ironically, this saves the morning for me; I get rid of stories.

Nea Kameni is a tiny two-kilometer wide volcanic island surrounded by steaming hot green-blue-brown water. People jump into its sulfuric bubbles for therapeutic results. The smell is profoundly intense; added to this, profuse cigarette smoking makes me feel I am on a bizarre Homeric journey of self-castigation or a dispelling of illusions for spiritual effect! I cannot believe I would experience detoxification in this water, for such a process is not just physical; my choice to not jump into hell's heaven inspires Iokaste's ire. I prefer to sit on the boat, which has blue walls and torn printed green curtains ... everything is taken to an extreme with fading red tables cracked and breaking. Sitting inside the cabin is as difficult as facing the hot steam outside under an already wide-open sky burning indulgently. Perspiration fogs my camera. My clothes are become my skin.

I do not feel like a rainbow.

What about me triggers her so? Maybe I do not need to know. She triggers me too.

After the party has bathed and burned, we step on the island for a walk. A landscape of big and small igneous rocks lie ingeniously in wild splendor in huge clumps scattered in divine order. I am driven to walk on them up a curving path towards a vast open space. His space feels surreptitiously surreal. I think of Michelangelo Antonioni's films, especially *L'Avventura* (1960), where Anna gets lost, triggering a search for her both on and off an island. I feel like Anna, but am not. I feel like more than Anna with a problem to solve—how to find my way to a more peaceful place on the island?

That place is in me, partly.

They want us back on the boat. I hear its gasping sputter weave between lava and steam. It's late afternoon, time for another story. Look at waves parting in agony.

We leave Nea Kameni, arrive at the tourist stop, disembark, and are driven to another small strip of beach. We park ourselves outside a small *taverna* set in a *grotte*, a cave. We are served potatoes and fish. The small party includes my hosts Iokaste, Zosimos, Vara and Otis, and some of their local friends; they converse in Greek. I listen to the chatter, the eating, and the waves. Not hungry, I snack out of politeness. Zosimos says if I do not love to eat, I cannot live in Greece because Greeks love food and all the rest that goes with it; he laughs. They like to drink; I don't drink. There is a further distancing in our relations.

To top it all, I am embarrassed to find that I have left my cards and traveler's cheques in my room in Athens. Greece is supposed to liberate me. Not carrying cash is liberty? The plastic card will save me.

We are at this beach for what seems like hours. It is good that I had already packed to leave their hotel for another one before leaving for the excursion to the land of solid lava. But it takes a long time for Leticia, wife of Telamon Balios, who is a friend of Iokaste, to come and take me to see the hotel where I shall spend the next three days. For now, I am at the mercy of folk I do not know, of elements I have to contend with, of my own inner chaos.

What strength must I find in me to deal with these demons, both external and internal? Silence.

Knowing their problems are not mine is grace; I am resolved to make the most of this dramatic action that seems to not really have a point at this time. Perhaps Santorini brings out all our demons; perhaps drama queens are drama queens wherever they are. Please, Goddess of Drama Queens, put them on stage, won't you? In some cheap vaudeville act! And please make it an intensely ecstatic comedy. Or take them home to your lair or sanctuary, lock them up in a big box and throw away the key. This is what my ally, my daimon says; I suppress a wee smile; a part of me is feeling small.

I recall our initial meeting, the time on the boat from Kea, the phone conversation in Athens! When people are overly effusive and "darling" others whom they have hardly known, it is wise to be cautious. It might be a sign of control or of superficial affection. Not wanting to judge someone so quickly, I had made a choice to join the family. I learn to listen to my voice and practice caution when it speaks to me. I am thinking these thoughts as I am brought to my new location, minus Iokaste and company. Relief and respite from the darkness of Greece collide with mine.

I recall a Greek-American I know in the safety of another shore noting that she has "so much to deal with, including being Greek!" She never did explain what it meant. Darkness of cultural identities also are revealed in slants of light.

Do you remember Maria? The dancer of old time? Dark shadows always hung around Maria's aging and delicate frame. Her voice had gathered a strange tone as if it came through a tin can with tears and self-justification.

Suddenly, in the rickety car she drove, she had turned to me, and, both woeful and laughing, said: "My mother don't looked at me as if I were real. All she would say was, 'Why this happen? Why I am here, torn from house? Why my family give me away? After all I had to do...?'" (She had shaken her head

147

vehemently.) "And it feel as if I given her away. But really ... I was the young then and Greece was in my bones. Still is ... and I'll never know what it is to live there ... so I have to deal with being Greek—that is a big thing. And live here..." Maria had been sent out of the homeland married to a man who could not care about anyone other than himself.

If I forgot to tell her story, I must be forgiven. Sometimes we travel as water under the bridge.

In the shadows of the land lie buried varied shapes of history. One of them is shaped like woman, the progenitor: raped, plundered, poisoned, avenger, avenged, daughter, poser, betrayed, betrayer, tenderer of the hearth, wife, mother, sister ... all this and more. Mostly the one who carried secrets of shadows of civilization's zest for life and ardor for dying, whose music strummed in her bones and chords ... even as Greece, this magnificent mythic being, was losing its dances to breaking of her land ...

Maria! Maria!
Where shall you root?
What fruit shall grow from your branches?
What music fall from your toes?
Do you see how the sun sets
over temples, between the hills?
Who will call you his own
when the night is done with you...?
For night will grind you away...one day...
and mother will be lost in the seas of another reality...

When people insist vehemently that they cannot ever be free, how can they even taste what they desire but remain shadows of shadows of shadows of old lands whose psyche is scratched with uncertainties? Aren't we all driven thusly in moments of fear, shock, vulnerability, when our sense of self is asked to break so it can rebuild anew?

The old car turns a bend. To my right is the Aegean, right in front a beautiful sun dancing to set. We arrive in Oia, beautiful Oia. My heart fills with delight at the flooding peach tones fusing with the blue waters.

Tall darkish handsome Telamon and his cronies welcome me at the simple resort, which is run by Cyrano Naos, ex-military, who resembles Picasso and insists on getting me *grappa*. I don't drink alcohol, so Telamon finds a way out of the situation. He exchanges our glasses, fills one with water and takes the grappa. We down the drinks. Cyrano asks me how it is. I say, "excellent." He is so happy that he brings me another one, smilingly watches waiting for me to sip and appreciate. I smile back. Yes, in a moment. *Efharisto!*

There is another sleight of hand as the guys look on with amusement. I have yet another glass of *grappa* to drink or to gripe about. This musical glass game has become fun. Cyrano offers to show me the rooms in his guesthouse. I say it is too remote from the center of town. But I take this opportunity to use Cyrano's phone to call Milos and pass on the message about the hotel to Selene and Lykaios—they had wanted to come and had requested I call and let Milos know.

When I call Milos, he laughs and laughs. It is joyful, this laugh. He tells me he went swimming and then had a drink with his friends. He was at the beach from noon until 5 p.m. I give him Cyrano's number. I feel glad to be here—yet a familiar voice comforts. I am feeling like a big sister.

Santorini is a lovely island, and I find out that, as on other islands, one needs personal transportation to get around. Buses are problematic; a car is preferred. But I am not organized for all this on the trip, and the wallet issue has thrown a pall on such development. Leaving Oia and driving into the town center, we watch the big orange-red ball we call the sun clip slowly into the sea. Sunsets are a treat for divinity.

Leticia drives me to the Hotel Anemomilos and leaves me by her car. It is strange, this remoteness of hers. I might find out why later when events unfold in their own way and bring me face to face with more of the unknown. I take my bags and walk to Anemomilos and meet Spiro the manager. He has a woman working for him show me to my room. It is nice and he will arrange with someone to use my American Express card, one that most people do not prefer. High rates or charges make this lovely blue formidable. But all is *entaxi* so far.

I am in room number two. The hotel is not quite by the sea, but one can see the sea from the balcony. There is a pool, which I enjoy swimming in. Across the street is the Kadmos Market, where I meet a man named Paion, whose insights about the island will soon help me gain a clearer perspective. He also owns and runs this market. I buy snacks and return to my room to eat even as I gaze at the sky. At dusk, I walk into Oia village downtown and find AurOra, Telamon's jewelry and gift shop, and meet Fedro, his cousin, and other relatives. However, the highlight is my meeting with Pippa with wavy dark hair that smiles in the wind, an Australian who has, as she herself says, "run away from home."

I am so happy to find someone with whom I can have an unhindered conversation in English that I feel suddenly liberated—yes, language is liberating, giving voice is liberating. A common language is freeing. I can express myself and be heard. "Do you mind if I complain?" I ask Pippa. Laughing, she says, "Go ahead." I am enjoying the sound of my voice. I have been silent for a long time. The tightness and feeling of suppression following my experience of Iokaste comes tumbling out of me—I will write about it.

Shades of Reflection in Oia

Recounting the day's dramas frees me in a way, from the silence inside me and from the chatter of my inner voices. I don't know which is foremost, but I am suddenly aware of the power of poetry and all the hidden stories that lie within: some waiting to emerge, some forgotten for all time like an ancient land and its mythos, some not needing the air of revelation.

I remember having said that Greece is buried, that ancient lands lie hidden in us. Mantras of the gods must remind us of our power to know our godlike selves. What else is life for? But to find our purity in the dross of civilization, existing in parts of places like Los Angeles, Rome, New Delhi,

London represent. Or other places: Athens. Here, Santorini, place for lovers...and Hersonissos, where I am to go in a few days.

But now Pippa, a friend for a few days, and I chat about life, about this and that. Most of all, we make jokes and laugh a lot, loudly and heartily. I feel happy. The bond of language and strange destiny brings us close for the evening. It is refreshing. We wait for Fedro to finish his work and lock up his store. They use seven huge locks on the door, a precautionary measure they take following a theft some years before. So wealth is guarded. There are seven ways to open a door; seven ways to lock it. Seven stars. Seven heavens. Seven chakras—Greeks love numbers! Indians do too. And you?

There is no serpent to protect here the wealth as in parts of India where folklore tells us that serpents make homes where people bury their gold. Perhaps a symbol for the *kundalini*—the serpent lying coiled containing the wealth of enlightenment? It lies buried until we dance to release the fountain from beneath rocks and experience the fountain rise up and beyond the crown to connect with Source. We are then flooded with essence, with Source.

Maybe essence pulls us towards air and light, a little like love, an infusion of one's self-hood with joy. Not so fortunate was the man Meander who moved hither thither in cyclic fashion for love of Hera but was made into a spring in the earth and forced for life to look for that which is eternal, even here on earth. Perhaps because Meander was denied by the fathers to meet with his true love, he is to weep for the hopelessness of the search, for the longing does not abate. What strange play is this of the gods that would deny him this fulfillment and keep a man lost?

His story tells me he is he in search of the feminine— spirit of god—a principle so desired in these times to bring balance to the earth and to our lives. The Divine Feminine suppressed for eons is springing up in places to remind us to honor Her so we may yet be revived and rejuvenated, and so we may survive.

Life processes reveal sets of interconnected systems in our physical, mental, spiritual bodies reminding us how closely we are in resonance with sets of interconnected systems outside us. We live with the continual flow of making meaning of experience in interrelated fields; we make stories to interpret what happens. We are manifestations of narratives, divine, profane, sacred shedding the skins of delusions for the skins of what make us happy.

The sound of our footsteps on cobbled paths creates a rhythm at nighttime that seems to be in synch with delicate twinkling of stars. The weave of conversation and laughter bring me back from reverie. We go to a *taverna* frequented by Telamon. He knows well the people who run it. At 1 a.m., it is well past my bedtime; I feel grit-in-my-eyes sleepy but go for the company and for tea. Telamon's Aunt Minerva (I wonder at her Roman name), around eighty or ninety, dressed in old lady elegance, has taken to me and keeps repeating how lovely I am and that I should stay with her the next time I visit Greece. I smile and thank her as I am touched by her warmth and learn to receive and perceive the bounds of hospitality. Will she be around the next time I visit Greece? What shall I say about her so I can remember her?

As she talks in this late balmy and sleepy night, she reminds me of our stereotype of wealthy Indian women, crusty and confident of their status. Perhaps, it is my bias from earlier times—bias against those very women with a facade that we used to think was hypocrisy. But it is not exactly hypocrisy; it is a carefully cultivated and guarded persona that comes from having to maintain conservative social relations and status. Of course, as idealistic college students intent on breaking out of social norms, we had thought of them in this way, certain we knew better.

There are many similarities between our two cultures, the Greek and the Indian; I am intrigued at images passing through my mind in an eidetic flow. The crusty voice made deep with cigarettes, the fashionably layered mascara and a way-of-the-world flick of the wrists. Woman endowed with the power of a dowager, loving to boss over everyone from behind a curtain of swirling cigarette smoke, is so in-your-face about how you should be in the world.

Feeling a sudden burst of energy, I make the evening become fun and gusty with anecdotes and laughter. But all too quickly exhaustion takes over. I ask Telamon to drive me back to Anemomilos. Pippa makes sure to remind me that "rest is very important" and that I, too, need it once in a while. I need it more than I've ever allowed myself. Too many demons keep me restlessly busy, getting nowhere. I promise myself to learn this daunting lesson of rest, a womanly thing: self-nurturing, pink, and hallowed.

Exploring Santorini

The next day I wake up feeling pulled in many directions. Desire to be witness to the beauty of this city conflicts with desire to take things with ease today. I think of a massage, but decide to continue sleeping; its power is anodyne. I imagine dragging myself out of bed to visit the town, and it does not feel pleasant. I decide to change my ticket and stay here one more day. Something about Santorini won't let me go.

In order to change my date and time of departure, I have to go to Thira.

Taking the bus to Thira is another adventure. No one is quite sure of bus timings. In a place where people know how to get somewhere, they do not know how to give clear directions. So with fits and starts, I manage to find my way into town, the part further away from the center. Here, the American Express office has moved twice, so I trace them to the new location and with a sigh of relief also find Pelikan Travels. I will be staying here one more day.

I drink lemonade walking along tiny streets, while all around me the blue sky spread serenely is unaware of how the heat affects us all.

I return from Thira and stop in the village of Oia to see Pippa at Windows, the gallery where she works. She's not there. Instead, I meet the owner, Ulrike, a lovely demure, somewhat fey-like, and endearing German woman. We share some good moments; I write a note for Pippa and leave.

153

On my walk back towards Anemomilos, I stop at the Blue Sky Taverna and enjoy a plate of fried *kalamari* and salad. The best fried *kalamari* so far, and the space is lovely, low-key, with a friendly waiter. I decide to have my last meal here before leaving tomorrow for Crete; then I walk back to the hotel for a nap. Feeling out of sorts and indecisive, I stretch in my bed and close my eyes.

I have taken a small hike around one side of the island near me, over and around rocks and mounds of grass that shoot down to the deep blue water. I have toured the street through the market, seen little shops, a donkey sitting in the middle of the cobbled street, quaint stark white homes woven into the earth and sky. I have spent precious moments marveling at the sea stretching all around for eons.

I have wondered at my wanderings: do I know what I seek?

Sleep and waking continually merge: sometimes I am not sure which stage I am in, so heavy is this sleep. I have to rouse myself from this underworld of dreams, or I will miss the party of the streets. I laugh wryly. Not being a party person in this moment, I feel lost from myself—my own voice a whisper inside me. It is not loud boisterousness I wish for—desire simmers in me for a voice, a reason, a wonder...a place on this earth to be fertile for me.

I take a long cold shower and walk back into the village.

Walking past Kadmos Market, I wave to Kailey, Irish wife of Paion, and see groups of people walk by all dressed in finery. They are headed for the big church in the main square for a wedding of an Australian Greek. Perhaps I can attend another Greek wedding. On the way I stop again to see Pippa at the gallery.

She is making her way through Homer's epic, hardly ironic here in Greece. Our seminar highlighted moments of the *Odyssey* as well. Here Pippa is courting the introduction, a complex discussion on structure and style. I suggest that she go straight to the story, then return to the literary discussion. But she believes she will understand the text better this way. Perhaps. Structures of texts may suggest structures of our lives as well and help us understand each unique style informed by beliefs and destinies, natures and co-creations. Surely we must walk our path with a smile in our eyes; today, I do not feel the smile in my eyes, nor in my heart.

We reach the church square. Pippa meets with Australian friends here for the wedding. Two little children are playing in the square; their fun is infectious, irresistibly. These rough and tumble little boys are being cared for by an older woman with very bad almost-no-teeth teeth, but her smile is a delightful expression of joy, simple painful joy. Yellow teeth can fall at any moment, in an instant. Will the tooth fairy grant her some unfulfilled wish?

Someone comes up and asks me where I have come from. They are Greek traveling from Greece and waiting for the wedding party. I say "both India and Los Angeles." Living as a hybrid, I say I am from both places; both places elicit a warm response from most people—again I hear we are related from a long time ago. The US is not a place culturally appealing to many; they wonder aloud how I can live there coming from an ancient land. I don't tell them how many Greeks I meet in Los Angeles. About my Greek dentist, about the wild man who jumps into his pool from a rooftop, about the aging dance teacher, about the woman who wooed a man with a red rose in her mouth, about my experience of the Greek Easter and the *epitaphios* at the local Greek Orthodox church.

The sky changes color—behind me is the laughter and chatter of wedding guests and tourists. The bride and groom arrive with their families; the party moves inside the church. I decide to change direction.

Pippa has returned to the gallery. Wisely and tenderly, she advises me to rest. Looking and feeling worn out, I agree. We think that we will meet at night. But once I get back to my room, I sleep from about 9 p.m. until 11 and wake up just to change into my nightclothes. It feels comfortably nurturing not to be walking around like a lost waif, aching in the back, wondering what to do next.

What magnets lie in Santorini rocks? Are they making me lose myself?

Tuesday morning on July 9th triggers a nice awakening. The world looks peaceful. I know Pippa must have realized that I slept through all the festivities we had planned. She will write to me and I will respond when I have returned to Los Angeles. She has said she might visit there someday. But we know such meetings are complete in and of themselves: they show up in vignettes, as messages, as windows.

I had asked her what her story was.

"Oh, you know, I was tired of the corporate stuff...!" she had said, laughing. So many of us are caught in the conundrum of the corporate world, or in doing things we do not really care to do. So we opt out for a while to "get things straightened out...to feel whole again." Unmarried and with no desire to have children, Pippa is free to go as and when and where she pleases. Santorini is a perfect place for her to rediscover herself, her longing, and her destiny: everything that makes her smile.

Far from home, I see islands secluded in the seas. Outsiders may corrode peace with their desires. For many it is a place of refuge. Locals know this and welcome us.

Woman with curls
runs into new walls
tunes of Aeolian harp

Santorini as a Vortex

There are many in the world like Pippa, the Australian on a retreat from her old life, who desire a shift in perspective for a sensibility that nurtures the creative living principle. Their spirit longs for a kind of home that is hard to find, so they find pieces of such a home in isolation in remote areas of the world. Perhaps, those remote areas are pieces of the self, waiting to be touched, seen, heard, loved, and made whole again. In such places, people meet others who have left their homes; such commonality creates space for dialogue, the search for and redefinition of self.

156

I had asked to lose myself so I could find myself. I remember this.

It is a beautiful island, but I wonder at the feeling of isolation this place reinforces. Perhaps, in the isolation, people feel they have found a community. That must be reassuring, but I'm not so sure. Such isolation also sings in big urban sprawls. It seems to be a symptom or condition of life when one feels a lack of cohesive sense of purpose or direction, or is in the midst of shifts. We think too much without thinking. Lack of clarity is the result of not being aware of wholeness.

But the air here is pure. Maybe this is the comfort, pure air in isolation. If you must be isolated, why contaminate your lungs? But smokers are aplenty in Santorini. I will not count how many ways people curl the smoke that leaves lungs for sea air.

The morning air invites me to the pool, from where I can see the big bold sea. By the pool, I practice yogic *asanas*, mainly *Surya Namaskar*—salutations to the sun feel so right. The ideal thing would be to just stay here and form a routine for some days of simple living—yoga, meditation, yogurt and fruit for breakfast, light walks, meals at the Blue Sky and making notes in the evening.

But I am running again; my ticket is for Crete and I must leave today. Santorini wouldn't let me leave yesterday. Its forces held me tied. Movement was difficult. All lines of the matrix had me in control. Today I am at peace; it is easier to move on.

Our thoughts keep us captive. Not all thoughts are captivating.

All packed and ready, I walk to Kadmos Market for my last breakfast. Paion is setting up for the day. It is always nice to chat with Paion; he has a quiet demeanor. He tells me a little about his life; he also tells me a little about me. He was into software technology, then into graphics design. But the ways of urban competition did not sit well with his nature. Many years ago, he met his wife who was in Greece on vacation. Their communication continued for some years; then she left her work in Ireland to be with Paion. After a year of working together, they married. The greatest joy, says Paion, are his children, whose "love is pure"—it is what he lives for. Working to support his family is easy; but other things are hard, like being a slave in corporate environments in crowded cities. It is time for companies to change their *modus operandi:* to work with principles of integration and transformation, where the work and the profits are for the good of all, not just a few. After all, where would they be without their workers and employees?

His tender voice goes soft when he mentions his children. Is it not also the sweetness and purity we long for that drives us to making children? Yes, biology and furthering the tribe. Paion sees in me such a longing. He said it doesn't matter with whom; one should just choose and make a home and grow in love. He says that I'd feel more rooted if I satisfied this longing, and then, traveling would become more pleasurable for me, instead of an adventure in search for the self. He notes that traveling would then be not a way to find the self outside the self but a journey one takes with oneself.

He shares stories about acquaintances who have experienced shedding the confines of their life through travel. It is true, he knows. He touches a nerve in me; I know he means well. I admit I still wish for the old ways but in a new way, that love be the foundation for a marriage and for making a family, not one to be forced by culture. But I have not met with that one, and I hold so sacred such a union that I leave it in my heart of hearts for that to unfold and I dream of it to happen. Thus far, my destiny has not revealed such a connection. I know many of us cannot live the same old life in the same way that others have lived and expected of us. So this sense of loss itself becomes a motivation to move out to define and create another grand plan. The cost is high; the prize may be worth it.

I think about Kailey, well settled and happy in her certitude. Both have helped me with small matters, my indecision, my confusion, and they have kept my bags between my checking out of the hotel until I take the bus to Fira. I promise to send Paion pictures that I have taken of them.

This discussion about Santorini is not over; we have barely touched the surface, but for now silence needs presence. Other than the island being a mirror of ourselves, I think the clear air fatigues us as it cleanses us. This, too, requires adjustment time, natural time of internal rhythms.

I ask him about the strange and disturbed man named Valentino who the night before had talked about the wonders of his Thai massage that "begins with the face and ends with the feet." He had suggested exchanging massage for energy work. Paion is not happy about Valentino's crude manners, apologizes to me for him. I learn a little about Valentino's background and his vagrant ways, lack of love in his life and, perhaps, despair. Sounds like many in the world. Who hasn't struggled and despaired?

Why should so many people go unloved when there are so many to share with? Why should every man become an island unto himself and wander floating with the lava around his heart solidifying into and by destiny's hands? Why should the softness of the inner chambers be corroded by crudities when our very purpose is to reveal the joy that we are meant to be, that we inherently are? Circumstances and choices often make people cruel. As our conversation unfolds, Paion shares tales illumining the mystery of the forces at play in Santorini.

This island, he says, is a mirror of what you are in essence and what you are experiencing at the time one comes to the island. He says this strange quality of Santorini has brought many to their knees. I note that I had been feeling very drained here, that the island was taking from me, that it wouldn't let me leave when I had planned on leaving. But today I decided that I would gather myself and come to terms with moving and not moving. Strangely, this had been my decision before this conversation as I swam and did yoga and sun salutations while the Bulgarian woman watched with appreciative eyes and swept the poolside. Paion noted that I give too much of myself, that this is what Santorini showed me by making me submit and stay. He says this is the power of the island and many people feel diverse compulsions in

159

different ways; they do not realize that island spirits call on their inner selves.

This is the island where people come to wed—do their spirits call them in?

Must we thank our mirrors for showing us the ache? Will I return to Santorini? Have we completed our journey together? I did not visit the site of the ruins, but I can leave in peace. Iokaste and family belong to the past; I move on away from ghosts. Recall my conversation with Milos about everyone being ghosts with whom we are completing part of our journeys. He didn't believe me or understand my thought. Ghosts are but memories, and we must choose which ones to savor, which release forever ... even as Odysseus traveled into and out of the land of Lotus eaters, the Cyclops, the Sirens—lands of shadows, voices of the sub-conscious.

I have two hours. Paion has given me plenty to ponder on. I also like that his name, which sounds gentle, means healer; his presence speaks well for the name. As he closes shop, promising me my bags would be safe there, I take my PD 150 and wander into the village of Oia one last time. Capturing lovely images or ghosts, I realize what a feast to the eyes is this meandering village, where every shop is unique in its own way; the architecture makes this place special. Many Santorini homes are built into caves converted into rooms using the concavity of these spaces and unique lines. One might say people in Santorini are cave dwellers, but with amenities that modern man enjoys. For us tourists, these structures are a curious delight, a cultural feast among others. Surely, for shops sell goods from Uzbekistan, India, Turkey, other lands as well as mainland Greece. Jugs, jars, icons, sculptures, rugs, replicas of ancient faces and Minoan art, seedy postcards, cheap Chinese made goods, South American souvenirs. It is an overwhelming indulgence to the eyes, rather like shopping in India. I buy a small magnet, a little temperature gauge on a Santorini house, for my old refrigerator back home.

Of course, what is breathtakingly beautiful is the sea just beyond—its blueness a powerful expanse to which one can only surrender something of one's self. It is captivating as are the mountains in the distance and parts of islands close enough to capture on film and far enough to remain moments in the mists of stillness. Sometimes this stillness reveals the poignancy of the ache, and its taste, an aftertaste.

A number of dogs rest majestically enjoying the glorious air. Some donkeys go by ready for passengers who wish to climb areas of Santorini, an island of mountains that rise in parts straight from the water. These creatures delight many people also trying to get shots of them. I am reminded of my little sister calling out as a child to the *"gunkas"* as she called them. Donkeys would traverse Pune (city of Shivaji, Rajneesh, and my old schools) streets with stuff on their back. Surefooted and cautious, donkeys have much to teach us.

Final Hours

Athinous, the port, is established where the base of the mountain rises out of the water. From there, the road has been cut in a fine zigzag along the side of the mountain to take one from the boats to the main part of town. The road is steep, but I have been on steeper slopes before. This rocky incline takes me back to the northern areas of India where now it is too dangerous to travel, for terrorists have been active claiming what is not theirs: ancient mountains of Kashmir, where arose consciousness of the principles of Shiva-Shakti, which is divine eternal union and dynamic creative force, and philosophy of *spanda,* bliss of vibration. These have melded landscapes with poetry of origins.

Our union is eternal and of cosmic proportions—a mathematically sound principle of harmonics. How and when shall the landscape of the heart awaken?

Athinous is a place apart from the rest of the island. It is here that I spend the last one-hour of my time on the island before taking the boat to Crete, the big island of natural wonders, gorges, Kazantzakis, Zorba, Knossos, Elounda, Chania—immense beauty and dross culture. Another adventure waits with watchful eyes.

The boat is called Flying Cat 4. We leave the shores at about 5:30 p.m. Carlos and Moon, fellow wanderers from Los Angeles, are also here. She is a seasoned traveler. Carlos does not know what to say about his transformations from this trip. Moon believes that she has already learned to take life more easily. Most Angelenos work too much, stressing on work more than leisure. I've heard this strain from many before. How laid back are the Greeks that, at a restaurant, they are not in a hurry to get you to leave or to pay them quickly so other customers can partake. You can sit as long as you like and savor time passing by, and in doing so sate the spirit.

I remember my last meal on the island at the Blue Sky: *gemista* with *xorta* and octopus, delicious and fulfilling. Spiros brings me *baklava* even though I do not ask for it—warm heart of a man being happy or being playful. I take pictures of him and feel badly for my not being able to eat the dessert, for I feel so full already. It is a special offering and I wished not to hurt his feelings! What if I could stay here longer and enjoy being fed! And make tourists happy with food!

Santorini memories are already tugging in my heart and mind.

But before I go I realize I must tell the story of Leticia, the Chilean married to the Greek. Leticia is a tall, well-built woman, strong and resilient. She has made her home in the community, albeit she is still seen as an outsider, so she tells me. Leticia and Telamon had met in Boston many years ago, were married and came to Greece. He is well established, so Leticia has no need to work, but she helps with the family business. They have two children, a boy and a girl.

Leticia has a solid and self-contained presence. There's nothing airy about her. She is grounded in her choices and moods. I ask her if she visits her family over holidays. The answer is "not really." Most Christmases are spent in New York because that is what the husband prefers. She has, in a sense, lost touch with her former life in Chile, with her family. There's no going back. With rare visits and very short ones, Leticia's Chilean heritage must now lie buried in her as the Yucatan lies buried in Mexico, as the stories of the stones in Greece lie buried in the dust. As we lie buried from ourselves.

Her children who know but a smattering of Spanish prefer to speak Greek for they feel isolated in Spanish. No one around them speaks it. So Leticia is alone again, but she is fluent in Greek. At the same time, she is the solid presence in her marriage. Telamon parties until late into the night, which means he sits and chats with people or dances, whatever. Leticia stays home to take care of children and other household matters. She smiles and agrees that 11 p.m. is a good time to be in bed. I prefer it too. I'm not a late-night person, primarily because I cannot sleep in.

With a flash of a smile, she nods, yes, she still feels like an outsider. I say, "But you are fluent in the language and you are settled here, why should you feel like an outsider?" She says she is not really accepted. I say, "You also look Greek...enough to not look foreign." She shrugs and says she is still foreign. She seems to be caught in a chasm: swirling between identities, unable to wear her Greek-ness and to deny her Chilean-ness. Identity is a strange concept. Perhaps if she kept better contact with her homeland, she might not be so much of a foreigner. Perhaps ... I have no easy answer.

I can relate to some of that. Born and raised in India, I live in Los Angeles but feel an outsider in both places. Yet I use the word "home" when I refer to either/both. This is how I resolve this issue. I ask if having a family of her own gives her strength and solidity that she might not have had if she were here by herself. She agrees—no one would uproot to move just to live in Santorini. Moving to Los Angeles is a different matter, and the US is a land of immigrants, which forces one to wonder about one's ethnicity, about one's cultural identity, about choice and circumstance. But she is a woman of passion. I think of Melina Mercouri in the film *Zorba the Greek,* playing the role of the maid who invites both scorn and awe.

I don't know why I sense shades of Medea, that says matter and spirit are different and that the life of the spirit is more significant than the life of material existence. How to live a life of passion? Where is passion without commitment of any kind? A commitment to live fully is dance of all possibilities.

I feel all spent; something about Leticia disturbs me. It must be her distance, her dark implacable eyes, and her grounded presence, which feels also somehow lost in moments when her eyes gather a faraway wistfulness. I wonder where this inexplicability hides. She is like the mother hen who drives her family in every way, while her husband is the breadwinner and player. At times, she must goad him to go to work while he sits and drinks *grappa* with the boys. When I ask her, "How many children do you have?" She replies, "Two...I have two." Good answer. I have liked, I think, her certainty of herself as a woman in charge of the family, if nothing else.

And her destiny! What of her destiny?

She has a dislike for and dread about visiting India. She said this is because someone showed her images of dead bodies in a river—odd to mark a whole culture from one image. I don't speak to her of the inequities I witnessed in my travels through Mexico, a land she loves to visit; it is not important for me to do so. But doors of my ancient land are closed to her; she has shut them down. Her destiny lies elsewhere, and she won't clear her karmic ties with India.

Leticia wishes me good fortune. I thank her. She is the last person with whom I have any communication as I wait for the bus to take me to Fira where I will take the bus to Athinous. It is not easy to feel close to her; her remoteness and reticence present a wall woven with care. Perhaps, that is why she does not feel she belongs here fully, even though she has a family, a husband, Telamon, and children. Perhaps, because she knows that the children, too, will leave as she did.

I wish her the grandest of manifestations.

I see her lone figure in a drama of epic conflict, standing inscrutably in the distance watching fires burn, turning around and going to her shelter to her brood, making sure they are safe. This is Leticia, or my image of her.

I wonder, too, what can happen to us as we leave home shores for foreign lands. While we form our destiny, uncertainties entertain us in strange ways. Sometimes, they can be magnificent. Sometimes, those ways are not kind.

Looking for Hira...

"Mi Mama, I know that you are anxious, but do not worry. I will call when I know. Please be calm. As yet, I have no new information.

Since I came to this strange place, I've had no rest. No one seems to know anything about Hira. But there is one woman I met yesterday who took me to her house. We sat and she told me something but I have the feeling that she was still hiding from me something. Something important. She said to me Sophie, her daughter, was friend of Hira. Both work together. They dig for stones and pieces of vases. You know how Hira love to work in dirt. You remember how she use to hide your precious things and dig them from the garden. You used to get so angry with her.

Don't feel bad. She said one evening Sophie and Hira went in a jeep with two men and one woman. She couldn't say anything to them since she was told they work together. With them was this one man she did not like. I think it is the same man I met yesterday...he is from many countries. I'm not sure from where he is. He says he has travelled everywhere. I cannot tell from where is his accent. But he was very smelly...of alcohol. He boasted about his good massage. I did not want to speak to him. But he laughed in my face and said, "Here, if you are not careful and if you are from another place, they make sure you do not get very far.... Or...they leave you alone. Very alone." And he smiled showing very dirty yellow teeth.

He then...well. I asked him what he mean. He said, "Your sister spoke this language quite good, but would not forget her place, her home. They wanted to make her theirs, but she always said..." and then he laughed. He would not say more. He...then he left the taverna.

165

I don't know, mama. I no understand. I wish Pedro was here with me. I scared I will lose myself while looking for Hira. Please pray for me. Tomorrow I meet with an official. They tell me he is an important man and kind. Don't worry, mama, I think that we can...I can find her...this place not so big...not so big as home, as our village. Don't you remember what Baba used to say—there's no place as like home. And Hira would tease him and sing, and this is where I will always come to sleep.

I think mama that Hira has gone somewhere else. To another place. To dig something new...I mean something else. I wish that she told us where she was going...instead of this silence for so long so many months.

Met an older woman. I feel she knows but I do not know what. She is strange. Something strange the old woman said to me. She said in her land, the women never complain. She said that they don't say anything because there is no one to listen. She said they must dress in black or people will paint them black and red and make them walk the street while other people watch.

Mama, can you speak to curandera, Pepita? Ask her to help to take next step. What should I do? I kiss the cross every night as you said me to do.

You know people here also wear cross all the time. They kiss it also. I seen it. They must be good people here. I think some of the people who create bad situations are like that man who is from so many countries...he has no country. He is from nowhere. No mama to love him; no friend or wife. That must be his problem.

Don't worry. Give my love to Papa and also to Pedro.

Your
MariaElena

Santorini tugs me in one direction, Crete in another. I must not look backwards or someone will be turned to stone. Maybe me. I turn my face towards the narrow space between the rocks. This is the path out of Santorini. If I stay here longer, I will always wonder about Crete.

How our forgotten
selves lie –
ache for a whisper
or a glance

So dissolution
resolves heart's song
which once was sung and lost

and becomes now
a Doric column
holding up a sky
that cannot fall

Is someone now listening
who was not then present?

"Of all the things, which wisdom provides to make us entirely happy, much the greatest is the possession of friendship."

~ Epicurus

Chapter 9 ~ Passage Through Narrow Spaces

As we pull away from Santorini, I feel a thrill arising in me of being on the high seas and traveling to the big island in the south Aegean. Made of four regions—Heraklion, Chania, Lassithi and Rethymno—Crete offers mountains, beaches, rocky coves, coastline, villages, antiquities, ancient history, and, of course, "modern" nightlife.

When we reach land, I feel elated. It is strange, this feeling, like something opened inside me. An Athanas associate, Pepe Glavan is there to pick me up. He's a tallish dark-skinned, grey-haired man in a multi-colored striped shirt. Taking my bag, he walks me to his car. I greet him who speaks no English. When we reach the car, he calls Athanas to say I have arrived.

We drive to the village of Hersonnisos. He gives me the choice of staying in the hotel or in his house. Because of the language barrier and desire for privacy, I choose the hotel. I'd feel more comfortable. He takes me to Hotel Eva. The next few days here are almost a nightmare, and I feel uncertain about my journey all over again.

But first I meet with his cousin, Vasilis. Rough on the edges, these folks enjoy the easy-going life, smoke generously and are goodhearted. Vasilis has a cousin in California like others whom I have met with some connection in California. Why not Arizona or Rhode Island, I wonder? It is the seas and the openness that draws them to this part of the US. They take me to dinner at a family style restaurant set away from the beach. Called Mano's, it is set on a small street that feels homey and familiar. The mother cooks daily in her kitchen, which serves wholesome cuisine.

Lyuba, Vasilis' Russian wife, and Manya, Pepe's wife, join us for the delicious feast, which includes fava beans, fava bean paste, octopus, *kalamari, tzatziki, dolmathes, dakos.* They are upset that I won't drink *retsina,* made right here on the island. Cigarettes cloud the space. I'll have to protect myself from smoke and the haziness in the air. My stock of lozenges, zinc and C's is diminishing.

The first night at the hotel is rough on my sleepy eyes and body. How can one sleep if people party all night into the wee hours, and then a new group of early morning players continue noise making, unaware that people might be asleep? This is not Germany, where civic rules are enforced. The noise is just one aspect that has me peeved. It is also awfully hot— the rooms do not have fans and the air is still. Sea breeze blows in another direction. Needless to say, I feel at odds with the universe. What have I done to land in this almost clean hovel? I wake up with a scratchy irritated throat and bronchia.

Hersonissos: the strip welcomes in its garish way. A series of restaurants serve the same foods and drinks and play the same kind of loud gaudy music. The strip does not please my sensitive spirit, but it is an eye opener. This place is a den of iniquity that appeals to variations of the baser instinct in people: young men haranguing barmen for sex on the beach; making bargains, the exchange of titillation for titillation. *Ohi, ohi,* I feel the voice of an erstwhile preacher arising in me. This place is for teens who have just discovered the spilling power of hormones and are out for a good time, or as Polidorus, a waiter at the Majestic, says, "with no taste, no mentality," as he tells me not to be upset at the Dutch boys being "hormone cool" making eyes at him. He makes me laugh. Kids are on holiday after finals, like, for instance, in Palm Springs, which is "sugar coated and new." Truly, Polidoros' comments and assurances make me curious.

Here I am by the sea reading Nikos Kazantzaki's *Report to Greco,* my recent purchase at a local roadside bookstore. I feel it imperative to read Kazantzakis on his native soil; I'd bought Edwin Rutherford's *Sarum* at a store in Stonehenge, UK, and read it by each ancient site I visited, including the Uffington horse in mist so dense I had to walk literally within two feet to see the white lines that marked the horse in the damp grass.

Polidorus notices the book in my hands, plies me with tea and asks, "You are reading Kazantzakis? You will understand what I mean what I say to the boys. I will hurt them if I have sex with them..." He shows off his strut and muscles rippling on his arms. I remind him that he had not said he'd hurt them but that he'd kill them. He laughs. "Passion...that is what it is...Passion...they don't know...but you will understand when you read this book."

"I don't need to read the book to know what you are talking about, Polidorus." I wonder at the visceral hint of violence in his boasting of passion. I know only earthiness, an expression of joy even.

Wherever people know the taste and smell of soil and its layers, where they know of ancient heroes overcoming the gods, of mating with their eternal beloved, there they are in touch with passion and raw emotion but also cunning and artistry. Perhaps, the Cretans are a bit like the North Indian Jats, a community who take law in their hands. Their passion is one of the solidity of the mountains, which meets the fluid sea to calm from time to time. Otherwise, they'd scorch in the fire, both within and without, and can cause much communal unrest. I am romanticizing the foreign here. As an outsider, I can do that, knowing that distinctions between self and other can be conveniently blurred or distanced. Can the real story be ever known when perceptions are varied?

However, what is extraordinary about them is that despite their symbiotic relationship with the Turks, they like to proclaim their unique difference. They seem to be organized in a collective consciousness that keeps them united in their struggle against the Turks although quite a bit of the language and cultural icons are influenced by the invading culture. We call Zorba famously as The Greek, but it is whispered that he was Turkish. So popular have been stories of Karaghiozis, main character of the shadow puppet of the Ottoman, that many Greeks like to claim him also as their own. Colonization produces a synthesis of cultures.

Hersonissos is a synthesis of a different kind.

171

All around me people drink varieties of cocktails with obscene names, which evoke laughter. The loud odorous environment disturbs me, so I plan hot days sightseeing and evenings lounging in the water. Since I do not drink, I can easily avoid the rakish bars. Instead, I enjoy my swim around 7:30 or 8 p.m. when it is cooler, the water refreshing, and the sky a gentle blue-pink.

Vasilis sits waiting at the *kafé* next to the Majestic Internet Cafe. I go over my plans for the excursions. Then I swim. I like the feel of water around my body. I feel free as I move against the waves, which are gentle, not like the waves in the Pacific, which are rough and strong. I swim out twice and return sated, as though a baptism had cleansed me of my first day here in Hersonissos, where the root *chakra* is all out of balance; I do not feel at peace here. But this is where I am landed.

I return to meet up with my hosts. Pepe has come to meet us. We walk to the tourist and travel center nearby to buy my excursions. I buy two instead of three. This is better, for Pepe will drive me to a couple of places in his rickety car.

At a supermarket, I buy sheep yogurt, which I enjoy for breakfast every morning. The market is called "Ariadne." The yogurt is set in clay bowls. I also buy a veggie burger. While the food in Greece is terrific, the vegetable preparations are limited. Everything is cooked with tomatoes. I admit I have tired of eating *xorta* and potatoes, fried *kalamari* and Greek salad, and even though I like *gemista* very much, there's only so much of it I can eat. But I like *gemista* for the rice in it. Some Greek women have insisted that I must eat more to gain weight. Why? I have asked with a smile. They sound like my mothers and grandmothers.

I tell Vasilis that I absolutely need a fan; the intense heat in the hotel room has kept me from sleep. He is not sure what I mean, so I draw him a picture of a fan. Ah, he says, he will ask a friend for the *misteria*. But he doesn't. Perhaps, my demands are tiring them, but they are not unreasonable. Clearly, my having to smoke with them is not to my liking, and I have to play a different kind of musical chairs to avoid breathing it in if I am downwind. This has already created a little distance.

My limitations make me recall words of wise Pippa, "Honor your body and your need to rest."

Day in Matala

On my second day in Hersonissos, I get ready early when it is nearly cool. But soon, the heat takes away my hunger; I am satisfied with a cup of yogurt with an apple. Not enamored of these strange and cheap surroundings, I leave as soon as I can for the bus stop to take the excursion to Matala further south.

Climbing up to the top deck of the bus, Giulia, a traveler from Italy, looks at me. I greet her, but she looks around, complaining, "It would be nice if we knew where we are." Helpfully, I say that it is nice anyway and find a seat across from her by the window. I want to see the changing landscape as the bus winds between hills and valleys. The remainder of Crete stretches far away from Hersonissos.

The bus stops at several hotels to pick up tourists for today's ride. Many Italians are on the bus; the guide will speak only in English and German. At Festos, they find an Italian guide for them. But first we stop at Gortys, which boasts of a wall with writing in Linear A, an early form of Greek. The guide tells us that "the laws of Minoa were very exact and accurate"; that "the laws of Minoa were fair"; that "the laws of Minoa were delivered by god himself to the king."

One of those laws pertained to rape. It is interesting to learn that if a woman was raped at night, the punishment meted to the man was lighter than if the deed had been done in the daytime. The reasoning behind this law was that at night, the woman also feels desire anyway, so she must have instigated the rape. I wonder about the definition and interpretation of fairness and of rape. Rape is rape, no matter what the time. Sounds like some laws in many lands today; where rape is concerned, the woman is the instigator, first culprit then victim. But if she is dressed alluringly, then she is asking for it. I am at odds with this "she asked for it" reaction. A woman is abused because she asks for it? Absurd what people do with shadow self and create laws to protect their incorrect thinking, which reveals lack of maturation and respect for life with no sense of what is just or right.

Rape or reporting of rape cases has risen, revealing a disturbing trend that shows men believe they have a right to do as they please. Some men think a woman dressed in a mildly revealing way is asking for it. Such immaturity and lack of respect are closely tied with patriarchy, which subjugates women while, at the same time, both promoting and condemning prostitution. Why should man believe women's job is to pleasure him?

A wise man knows it is the other way around. That woman's feminine spirit awakens him, encourages his masculinity to participate in life with honor and courage. He knows violence cannot inspire lovemaking; it demeans the human and sexual act. Wise man surrenders to wise woman.

As we leave Gortys, I think about desire, the good desire, creative desire, sensuous desire—is it reserved for the night? I smile at all those day moments when my flights of fancy and longing longed in daylight to connect with the man-right. I remember words of my poet friend in Los Angeles, how she sublimates her desire through reading other poets and taking walks. I wander into the poetic again to discover how desire dances with seaweed ... I remember this poem I will compose for her in her longing.

Swim not in the sea
for it reminds
of man juice

while sand particles
stick to skin
like longing

that does not go away

174

Swim not in sea
where languorously
plants wander round legs

and satin-mushed fruit
of desires
spiral up your limbs
and then down
like tears...

Swim not in sea until
you are ready
for blue-green

invitations of waves that
rise at pre-dawn
as sun-in-spoons

and arms spun like
well-worn time
encircle

what's left after the dreams
dissolve and love
has had

its way! Then only swim
in the sea. Only then
swim as two
can be...

Sotiris, the driver, stands ready by his bus, eager to get us all moving on. Susana, the guide, bids us hurry. I walk around some bushes and become aware of a harmonious cacophonic orchestra from the trees. Standing quietly, I listen a smile staying close at the many sounds of desire. *Tzitzigas* abound aplenty. The singing, the humming does not stop. It continues. Sometimes, it's almost a scream. These blind crickets sit on tree trunks gazing at nothing at all and make noises; perhaps they are bringing something to light. I do not know. Or they are crying for the light. I like to think so. Imagine walking through a forest filled with crickets.

We move on. Susana is rather aloof and sometimes gruff. I think she has done this far too long and the work, now a habit, has begun to pall. The driver Sotiris, on the other hand, is a pleasant chap. He has apologized two or three times to me already for not making a stop for me when I needed it. I said it was okay because we did stop when I so desperately needed it. He had turned to Susana who had said it was okay to stop. What bliss it had been to go out in the fields and squat; squatting is an art of freeness: the fragrance of golden liquid meeting earth, leaves burning in the sun, little rivers meandering, blue skies staring from above, such lightness, such bliss following rainfall. Such opportunities are rare.

Desire is color of golden, fragrance of wet earth...!

Time's Intruder

Soon we arrive in Phaistos, also called Festos, an ancient Minoan city, which as is recorded was destroyed in a late Bronze Age earthquake. The landscape is rugged, green, and expansive. The sky is filling with grey clouds. What wonder if rain were to grace us today! It rarely rains in the summers I learn. In India, July and August are months of rain; this is when peacocks dance and lands glow green. India has five to six seasons.

Needing quiet, I prefer to walk away from the group. Suddenly, I lose the desire to listen to information on what space was used for what in antiquity. All I hear in my inner ears is the song, "*Is mod se jaate hain../kuchh susta kadam rakhke, kuchh... /Pathar ki haveli hai...aashaon ka pani hai...*" (We move on from this corner, some with slow steps, some with fast steps... this is a house made of stone...these are waters of hopes desires...), an old lyric from the film *Aandhi*

176

(storm), with scenes set in the ruins. *Pathar ki haveli* = house of stone; *aashaon ka pani* = waters (tears) of hope. I also see images from an old Hindi film, *Lal Patthar* (1971) with Raj Kumar with nostalgia and melodrama of a long time ago when people heard songs in the winds and wrote their stories in stones. Today we decipher stories from stones, and then transfer them onto chips of sand and glass.

I feel like an intruder between passages of Time; I feel like a wayfarer wondering who and what I am. Wondering why I am here. I feel sentimental. Miss the dust of home and all that has gone before me. I wonder what is to come. Red dirt. Monuments. Love. Mythos. Nostalgia. The present does not exist. It is never meant to. It is a passage

Rocks and dust tell tales. We are trying to figure them out, these lovers in rock. *Patthar ke sanam.* Lovers made of stone. Cold. Distant. Voices are frozen in time and the heart! Where are the laws of the universe? These laws that speak about balance of the heart, that make layers of meaning known to us; these laws that bring the right songs to our lips, the right thoughts in our minds. How and why we get so out of tune, out of sync with our sacred inner selves?

An incurable romantic, I like to believe in the goodness in people. I do not wish to know that they are lacking in romantic spirit or imagination's sweet kingdom. That is my *hamartia*. Only sometimes do I realize that the innocence and purity that I see in people is not always theirs, but my projection. I wish it were not so. I seek it everywhere and walk gullibly into situations where I need protection. Perhaps, I need to also give up expectation so I can see what truly shows up and allow for my growth in true ways.

How can we all be true to the spirit, to love, to joy, to all? Simply by just being; such a choice requires an instant change of attitude and mindfulness.

Are we instantly enlightened when we so choose? Perhaps more true to say it is a processional unfolding; the moment of choosing is a decision to embark on this process. That tree over there does not have these questions—it is always true to its nature. We are not always so. What does it mean when people say, "Be yourself!" Who are we but that—

177

we dear besotted creatures unique and undivided, unaware of ourselves? We need to recognize ourselves with new eyes.

I buy a book titled *The Secret of Crete* by H. G. Wunderlich to know more about Crete and the shared pre-Alexander heritage. Gazmir Aeolus, an associate of Athanas has insisted that all life comes from Crete, the Dravidians are Druids; that there is no such group known as Aryan; that all languages come from Greek; that the *swastika* stands for four words beginning with *gamma* (from which if reversed, we get the *swastika* as we know it); that my name, "Ambika" suggests a kind of *amphora*, hence womb, hence mother. In Sanskrit, "Ambika" is Shakti suggesting Saraswati (knowledge, wisdom, culture, et al), Durga (the strength of fortress, the warrior), Parvati (Shiva's Divine Consort), and even little mother, and she is Mother of Creation itself.

Is Greece liberating me from myself?

I am not sure that all Gazmir's conclusions are sound; when I check with my teacher, Dorothea Kenny back in Los Angeles, she pooh-poohs it. But stories illumine something; in some people, it is the desire to see their land as supreme over all others. This is dangerous. In others, stories suggest their own search for permanence, sometimes fruitless. Or for something else not yet identified.

We move on to Matala, where we will eat lunch and some will swim. I know I won't for, in this surreal heat, I am already burnt beyond recognition. I choose to sit at the restaurant, where the heat will slowly saturate me. But I can be in the shade and I can drink glasses of water.

The Italian Giulia and I feel sharp pangs of hunger, so we sit at this almost deserted restaurant. She orders chicken *souvlaki*; I ask for sardines and salad. Canned sardines don't make the cut. The fresh fried sardines with fried potatoes taste so delicious, I can hardly imagine anything tasting this good anywhere else. It belongs there, in Matala, in that time. It cannot taste the same anywhere else. It cannot even be called sardines and potato anywhere else. It won't be true.

Again, our conversation goes to her problems. I can't contain myself any more. I tell her about my travels in Greece, a little about the wallet, about learning to appreciate what we have, about learning to say, *"then pirazzi!"* What an apt phrase Seamus had taught us; it comes in handy. A bit dismayed that I diverted attention away from her tale, Giulia gets up, says she is ready for a swim and leaves. I am the only guest in this very big eating room, where the sun pours its indulgent self on vacant tables.

Kafé Nero and More Predictions

The waiters, Damoulis and Baska, hover around me grinning. Damoulis—tall, dark, and handsome in his own way—points out the similarities between us. We are the same, he says, as he places his arm next to mine. But he is darker and a wild flirt. I remind him about my request for *kafé nero*. He looks at me, grinning, and then brings me some. In the meantime, Baska is making goo-goo eyes at me and sending me kisses from across the room. I wonder if I should have gone swimming after all. But they are harmless, I decide.

He comes to the table and looks at the book that I have with me, *Greek for Tourists*. His hand, however, is by his crotch, and he is nervous. I find it all so funny; in fact, I want to laugh so hard I think it might offend them. Or I am scared it will encourage him. I know he is not really reading the book; he is too nervous to do so or he cares less. I am sure that his brain is on overload as his desire simmers in him, bursting at the seams of his ridged skins. His hands are shaking. I am not going to jump in the hay with him—there is no hay here. *Then pirazzi ...pirazzi!*

What can I do? Is he not the story and also the hero of this story? Along with the sardines, the coffee and my sitting with the book, I watch the drama unfold on a reality screen as I think of the 1963 film, *Young Aphrodites*, directed by Nikos Koundouros: 200 BC, nomadic shepherds by the rocks, young and virile, running after a young girl and a woman with the lute in deserted places. But the girl is raped and the shepherd throws a dead bird in the sea before allowing himself to be swept away. Brutality of the imagery is stark.

179

This place seethes from the ground up. What would happen if this scene I am living were a movie shot on location highlighting the mythic consciousness of the Greek wilderness, romanticized, devastated, and now transferred to celluloid. Baska, *bas!* Or you might become a *bas-relief* for a museum. I nod smiling and talk about the book. I do not know if he understands what I say. Then hearing Damoulis walk up the stairs, Baska turns to leave.

Good, I'll never know if he smelled like a man or a messy sweaty over-boiled soiled kitchen.

Damoulis returns with the coffee. I drink it—it's good, really good, like coffee of the gods. Then I pour the grains into the saucer. He is thrilled I know about this custom. We take it down to his mother, a short nice looking woman with grey hair. She reads the coffee grounds and says, I will go and come back. I will marry a man with black hair, not rich, and have five children. This is all bogus, I know. So I ask about another man, someone I make up. She says, yes, the other man is better. That one will be good. Okay. I'll wait for that one—who wants five children only to be left high and dry with all the work, although I do not think that would be my fate. Damoulis insists she is accurate. Yeah! I smile and nod, imagining that he was imagining the part that makes the babies. Just that!

Another story for another time, as they are all accurate, aren't they? I should know better. It is now time to go to the bus. I realize when I reach it that people are already heavily ensconced in their seats. Giulia has saved a seat for me. She is all burnt, but smiling. I am glad she looks happier.

We are on our way back and driving round one of the bends when a car runs into the bus. The car driver is clearly at fault. Naturally.

I see this as one more opportunity to use the fields; this is a natural bathroom break. We are here for more than an hour with the police, whose investigations are a series of loud questioning and repartee.

Then begins the final drive back home. Giulia says we paid for Zaros and we are missing it. Smiling, I remind her that we did not pay for the accident and we experienced it. This playful banter between us is not over. When we are close to my get-off point, she says she will e-mail me. I have many ghost e-mails waiting for me when I return to Los Angeles. But I don't get any of them. Not even from Pippa.

It is about 8 p.m. when I manage to get a swim in the sea. My old grocery store has run out of the terrific sheep *yaourti*, so I buy one that is a blend of cow and sheep, and, for a change, find a veggie burger for dinner.

I must sleep earlier than usual even though I don't have a fan. I excuse myself from the gathering with Vasilis and his wife. Instead, I sit with Helina, a German waitress, who has been very kind. She longs for India—like so many I have met who dream of India. I, too, dream of India, blended with one in my imagination; it is what nostalgia does. Helina is here to repair her life from a divorce and complications. But what is lovely about her is her joyfulness, in spite of her many travails.

At the hotel, I move to a quieter, not cooler room. Night turns restlessly burning away karma, or gathering some.

Like many nights
whose stars travel to world's edge
my dreams wander...

bending upon trees
roots drown in themselves

spirit of land
calls without calling
whose eyes sink into flesh
and abyss awaits...

Like restless nights
sheets unravel my skin

story cannot wait
she takes night
into her eyes and bids

you write the pure word

181

fingers paint on skin
your colored skins
so tribes command

wear the right shoes
sleep in the right bed

arms are not an abyss
gaze into my eyes
how silence stretches

weaves longing of ages
my eyes – your eyes – ours

the only map home...

In Search of Zeus' Cave

My third morning in Crete is like my second, except that I am on my way to Kera Monasteraki, Dikteon Andron, with the last stop at Aghia Nicolaus. It turns out to be a remarkable day. I am, however, glad that I'd bought two excursions. I'd thought I would spend three weeks writing on a Greek island, but it hasn't happened.

The drive to Kera Monasteraki, which is now a nunnery, is pleasant even though I have moved around in the bus a few times. I tell the driver, Taxerio, that I am returning to my seat in the front and that I had gone to the back because of the smoking. He laughs and calls me *"Kukala mou..."* He is drawn to my playful spirit. I like the sound of the word, *piraktiri.* And *kukala mou* from him sounds sweet. Makes me smile. Stefani, our Swiss guide, will share brief anecdotes with us along the way. We are almost at this monastery, which has seen much action and is home to a miraculous icon of Kera (Our Lady).

Built with stone between 961 and 1204 CE, Kera Kardiotissa Monastery is in a charming wooded area. Home to an icon of Panagia, Mother Mary holding the baby Jesus, its inner walls are darkened with time and soot, and we may not take pictures inside. This very special place has suffered many attacks by the Turks, who nearly destroyed it, but the Kera was restored to become a center of the local province during Cretan revolutions. This Byzantine monastery is dedicated to the Nativity of Mary, celebrated on September 8, Virgo for the Virgin. The frescoes along the walls have a quiet beauty in shades of yellow, like parchment at times.

An interesting anecdote tells us that a merchant stole the miraculous picture of Kera and moved it to a church in Rome in 1498, the year that Constantinople fell. Soon after, a copy of Kera was placed in this monastery in Crete and also came to be considered to have miraculous assignations. More recently thieves stole even the copy but were arrested. Yes, she is miraculous. Yes, we all make wishes expecting miracles.

We may make wishes, and if they come true, then we must return here to tie a metallic icon, a symbol of what we had asked for. Such practices occur in many lands. In India, we find near *dargas* and temples, people tie threads on old trees for the same reason. Trees remain patient witness to human desires, through which people hope to see miracles appear in their lives.

How similar are our cultures in so many ways! Folk connection with elements is universal; this sensibility informs the creation of beliefs and customs the world over. Perhaps this is one reason why we find so many overlapping synchronicities in our diverse cultures, where traditional thinking lurks to pull one away and into sometimes pleasing or queer acceptances and indulgences.

I rather enjoy being inside this monastery painted in shades of yellow, ochre, soot. But we are on schedule to drive through Lasithi Plateau and onward to the place where baby Zeus was kept hidden, so he may be saved from the wrath of the father: new orders taking over the old system must contend with torture or banishment or hide and be renewed, but they must survive.

183

In Cave of Possibilities

From Kera, we go to the Dikteon Andron, the mythical birthplace of Zeus. Since his mother, Rhea, lost all her babies to their father, Kronos, who would eat them up for fear of being usurped and lose his position as the king of the gods, she decided to save this baby and hid in this cave to give birth. She was successful. Later, Kronos found out and demanded the baby be given to him; instead, he was given a rock wrapped in cloth. He swallowed the rock, supposedly one of the *omphallic* stones in Greece; it has its place in Delphi. One other such rock is in the island of Delos, the birthplace of Apollo. The sun rises over Delos and, magically, you see Apollo is born.

> *Sun rises*
> *in your haloed eyes*
> *I am born*
>
> *gaze of your eyes*
> *gazes into mine – in another's*
> *language is born*
>
> *would single eye*
> *undivided univision*
> *have saved the world?*
>
> *would there not*
> *have been a world*
> *without two or more?*

Light must invite balance and clarity, which leads to harmony. What must be the metaphor for our post-modern age, for our times now that we have diverse forms of laser technology and machines that test the speed of atoms; now that we have learned to harness nature and, more than that, now we have harnessed energy for our destruction? What must be the story to save humanity today with all that we have come to know and to love and to desire? What is the story that we need for our renewal? I am asking for something specific, something concrete.

When we ask questions, answers must be inevitable, reveal themselves. I shall wait, but not for long. When we phrase our questions rightly, an answer is evident. When we begin with an answer, the question must be illumined and the way clear. If we know deeply enough without chatter, we receive truths, fundamental to our nature and existence.

When Gandhari, daughter of King Subala of modern day Kandahar, wed Dhritarashtra and discovered he was blind, she blindfolded her eyes to experience his way. After many years when the blindfold was removed, her eyes were sharp as lasers. The silence of her eyes had concentrated power to see and to burn another at will, so some say. What of Clytemnestra, also a seer, how did truths come to her? And the blind seer Teiresias, how did he remember visions he spoke of? The Delphic Oracle unveiled offers no solutions but presents us with choices. In other places of religion, politics, and commerce, truths were veiled; answers are left to the unwary population.

Why do we so readily enter the world of shadow and illusion and live with lies? Does Valmiki know after having written the great *Ramayana*? Is there a way out other than bowing to the gods? Chanakya cleverly devised ways to subdue enemies in his *Arthashastra (Science of Wealth)*, his treatise on money and politics, but he showed no way out of human weakness. The Catholic Church offers space for confessions and dispensations but no resolutions. Not even diverse world councils have practical answers to shadow and conflict. Old counsel has not worked. The plethora of spiritual leaders and great ideas have influenced people but not yet transformed systems; superpower politics has wrought dissension and destruction; the aware among us ache for pure reason, love, and grace to regenerate will and imagination.

The answer must be somewhere in us—shall we insist, intend, and collectively activate our awareness and the dynamic to live with reverence. What if?

185

I recall my starry-eyed idealism and telling my students when I first started to teach that if each of us the world over would synchronize our clocks and, at a designated hour, pick up a flower and breathe in its fragrance all at the same time with clear "intention" of inviting "goodness," would we not connect with collective group consciousness and make transformation happen right then and there? I had received looks of consternation, and maybe even a touch of awe hovering over a "you're weird" expression.

Some people might see those of us who see through veils to be mad or eccentric; to some others, it is ordinary state. I remember feeling that pure consciousness is not heightened state but ordinary state of awareness.

Now it is time to descend further into the dark—the place of creative indulgence, sacred places of the Goddess where she hides her treasures.

Exploring Dicteon Andron, the Womb

So here we are outside Dikteon Andron, which is also called Psychro Cave for its proximity to the village of this name in the Lasithi Plateau. This remarkable cave is on the northern slope of Mount Dicte.

Stepping foot in a place where Zeus was birthed is phenomenal. Zeus: god, king, commander, shape-shifter changing from man to swan from man to bull, being thus both anthropomorphic and theriomorphic, was willful, arrogant, proud. Whatever the spirit desires, it self-creates to emerge in new form. Avoiding the story of the rape of Leda and Europa, my intention is not to let Zeus off for any dastardly deed, for these persist in horrific ways today, but to note the coming into new form of old forms by some sort of renewed synthesis, willing or otherwise.

The descent into the cave at Dikteon Andron is intriguing. I learn that *Andron* is a space often found in privileged Greek homes set aside mainly for men's entertainment. It was inappropriate for women to enter this space. *Andron* suggests male, manly, brave, virile in Old Greek,

186

and variations of this word appear as names in Nordic and other languages, becoming Andrew in English. In Hindi, *andar/antar* suggests inward, inside, interiority. If *Andron* is space of man and, referring to an Indo-European linguist connection, *Andron, Andres, AendaaR, Andru* et al., is akin to the name "Indra," Vedic god of Thunder, then I wonder if Andron here suggests both interior and male. Thunder and rain are symbolic sperm from the skies: they make fecund; they impregnate and spark life.

But the cave is also womb where inner outer worlds connect to make whole, to make new form. So entering the cave really means Rhea entered her mother or grandmother. Native Americans like to call this space "Grandmother"—in ceremony, we sit in a dark teepee; this is Grandmother space. In India those seeking a new reality, an inner journey, leave city cares behind to live in caves for a renewal. We renew in the hearth, in the cave, in the heart.

With awe in my heart and curiosity rippling in my being, I enter this ancient space. I am in the midst of stalagmites and stalactites of various sizes, rich with mineral encrustations, and layered with memory of ritual and worship since antiquity. Down below is a shallow pool, which rises after the rains. Walking in here requires care and attention as the steps are small and can be slippery. Clearly this space, kept together with metal railings and pathways with stairs through the five antechambers, had been well used first as a place of burial or ritual, but also as shelter by local shepherds.

Before I begin the journey in this cave and down through its many levels, I see people throw coins into the lake below, as they do into potages of water to invite blessings into their lives. It's the same here as elsewhere. Between many stalagmites that form wildly beautiful pillars in the cave is a fascinating landscape—like, perhaps, the chambered heart, valves, veins, arteries and all. Blessings will be remembered and the heart assuaged. Perhaps, what they wish for will bear fruit. Was it not here where baby Zeus was protected from the wrath of Kronos? Where time stopped.

The inspiration of worship here was the Diktaean Zeus who, as the story goes, died and was reborn each year.

Chants and hymns sung here called for peace, prosperity, and justice. We are still calling for these virtues in our lives and in our polity. One must walk in this cave carefully for the edges and steps are slippery; as one navigates modern life where politicking is slippery and creating life of harmony highly desired. Especially now more than ever!

Emerging from the cave, I wonder what it must have been like for pregnant Rhea to hide from Time itself away from the light in the damp darkness of the cave. Does the darkness hide Time? Or contain it? When you light a lamp in a dark room, does the clock start ticking? Here, too, Mother Kali stirs me as a pebble rolls along a rough edge: still or in wild waves, Time just is in and beyond us and in our machinations—we are all that and nothing.

The sun never stops its movement in the skies; the Earth never pauses in her rotations as she invites the sun to different parts of her body. It is intensely hot; the sun needs no invitation.

I return to the bus stop and drink a two-euro Lucozade. Everywhere I have paid eighty to ninety cents for this refreshing drink. But this is well worth it and perhaps not enough. Taxerio asks me if it is okay for him to smoke. I smile—why not, what can I do? He laughs. When everyone has returned from meandering, we board this rumbling bus and drive away in search of a restaurant.

A couple of hours later we are in a valley of windmills; we find a restaurant called Anemomilos (meaning "windmill") like my hotel in Santorini. The food is passable. I sit with Kitten, a young woman from Hong Kong. A German woman takes a picture of me with my camera beside the blue and white pottery; I think she isn't focusing quite right. I hope I am wrong. We leave for Agios Nikolaos, a city that rests on a prior Dorian city, Latos pros Kamara.

The spreading town of Agios Nikolaos is refreshing, clean, and beautiful. It is no wonder that it has drawn the attention of artists and filmmakers over the years. There is a touch of the quietly extravagant here that lifts spirits. But we are here for just one hour. A walk along the quay and into the market brings me to little shops. Truly a clean town—it feels liberating to be here. I buy a yellow skirt and a small white crocheted T-shirt. We have to rush back and are hustled into the bus in just about an hour for our return to the sodden degenerate Hersonissos, but as I write about these days, my affection stirs.

Taxerio suggests that he won't drop me off but take me to Irakleio for Cretan dancing; it is a wish in passing. Our guide on this trip, Stefani has been very pleasant. In a moment of reaching out to me, she mentioned her husband had died from drug complications; I sense there is more. I do not need to know; she does not need to tell me. I respect this reticence. A beautiful drive along the northern belt of Crete brings us back to our respective stops. The day is done.

Tonight, I will have a fan. I make sure to call Pepe and explain what I need. When we meet, I draw a fan on a piece of paper. His eyes light up, "*Ah, misteria!*" he says. He brings me one; it is a relief! A little mystery and a mist maker, and now I have this contraption with rotating blades.

I again ask myself what I am doing here, what is my lesson. I have no inkling what will unfold. Surprises happen when we let go of very tight schedules. Doorways open to new perception.

Off to a Resort

Saturday presents a lazy morning. After breaking fast I return to my room. I wish to write, but there is only one plug point; I choose the fan and nap. When I wake up, I call Nestor K., an acquaintance twice removed, who I had thought was in Xania. But he is in a small town by the sea near Aghia Nicolaus. He has just passed by Hersonissos and will pick me up on his way back from Irakleio. Terrific. I change my plans of driving through mountain villages with Karajas for my last day.

I am waiting at the curb when a red sports car drives up and stops by me. It is Nestor and his friend, Althaia. Together, we drive towards their resort near Sitia. Nestor is a medium height well-built man with dark curls. His friend, Althaia, is an exuberant petite woman studying contemporary

189

art. On the forty-five-minute drive, Nestor tells me a little about his resort home owned and run by his parents. By the sea await many treasures. The biggest surprise of all awaits me in his home.

We enter the house and greet some people in the foyer. I shake hands with an older man but we are not introduced. We walk onto a landing and then downstairs to another room to drop off our bags. Then Nestor casually remarks that the man upstairs is Angelopoulos, and I might be interested in meeting him since I have an interest in film.

Theo Angelopoulos, the great film director, is in this home! I have been deeply interested in his work for some years. In fact, we were to have met him on the screenwriting trip with Seamus. He must have returned then from Moscow.

I carry my camera bag and return to the living room. Before I can even make contact with Angelopoulos, I have another surprise. American actor Harvey Keitel is on the landing with his wife and the Angelopoulos couple. Keitel looks at me, says, "Ah, Madam, how are you?" and proceeds to descend the stairs. We shake hands and make small talk. He tells me he has finished reading a script by an Indian writer that deals with the issue of terrorism; he likes it. He wants to know a little about me. I tell him I live in Los Angeles and am a teacher and poet. He introduces me to his very young wife who appears in a white bathrobe. They are to leave in some hours. He does not want to be photographed. He has enjoyed his time in Elounda. We say goodbye.

I am excited and eager to approach Angelopoulos, a balding man of medium height and slight build. His wisdom rests layered in his wiry self. He must be in his sixties. I tell him this is "pure destiny." He laughs. We speak the same language in meaning. I tell him that I was part of Seamus' group and that we had missed him, Angelopoulos, during the film-writing seminar, as he was in Moscow when we were in Thessaloniki and returned to Thessaloniki when we came to Athens. He smiles, says, "I promised Seamus that I will meet the group when I return from South Africa...I went there after Moscow." I say, "I'm the only one of the group left in

Greece...so happy to meet you." I ask if he has five minutes for me. He nods.

We walk to another house at the resort and wait for his wife, Phoebe, to join us, as she will translate for us. She has long tumbling wavy reddish hair and a wide smile. We speak for about fifteen minutes. I am moved that he shares almost the same things in essence that I believe and understand and that I was going to ask him. I say that his works have an epic depth and scope even though they do not follow epic conventions. He acknowledges, adding that, indeed, his intention is to make epics. I suggest they are interior epics. My heart is racing with excitement.

He says that all his writing and filmmaking are about looking for home, about coming home. It is about the longing to create or recreate what was so to speak in ancient times—the glory and the nobility of the human being in divine wisdom and humor. These are my words and I find his thoughts are so close to my own that I next want to ask him about the transformative power of his body of work. No sooner than I think this than he proceeds to speak about transformation. He speaks in Greek; Phoebe translates. In spite of the language barrier, I find a face, a soul that mirrors my thoughts. We are poets. I tell him I feel the same poetic sensibility as he in his perception of the world—despite our sense of intra-connectedness, we remain in search.

We are in quest of our innocence.

Of course, he has been in the business for many years; I am a novice. Not the business of poetry, but of envisioning and creating cinematic poetry—the kind that shatters belief and creates new meaning.

The poet always needs new words and new lines. The poet connects with the world through diverse images, so we belong even in our passionate and necessary transformations. It is inevitable. Poet is a filter of consciousness. So Angelopoulos notes in his film *Eternity and a Day,* about which he speaks very lovingly, for it is a story of an aging poet in search of his eternity. This he finds in the innocence of a vagrant Albanian child who gives him words that he had forgotten or not deemed significant.

191

I thank him for his time, his wisdom, and his passion. I will have to watch the film again in order to remember more of what he said. Though I have been occupied behind the camera, I feel elated and gratified by our interaction and our similar perspectives on the mythic self, lived and loved, known in journey's narratives about life's cycles.

The rest of the day is restfully pleasant at this wonderful resort. I sit by the sea with others. We eat and then they pair up to play backgammon. I watch. They go wind surfing. I watch. We return to the house. When the sun sets, I go for a swim. The water here is rougher than in Hersonissos but lovely, invigorating. Then I come out of the water, I am told there is a party. The guests have arrived; I dress up in casual attire (it is all I have brought) and I join them on the lawn.

Many journalists both French and Greek are here to experience their inner time expand; it is what a resort is meant to do, notes one of them. This is a business cocktail hosted by the Thermopouloses. Nestor is nowhere to be seen, nor is Althaia—they have disappeared into the inner recesses of the house. His sister, Martina, and her boyfriend, Paolo, hang around at the party, but I speak with some of the guests. Nestor's parents are coolly detached—it is a nice party. "Nice" seems to be the word of choice in its ease of use, respectful and aptly distant for the occasion.

A British Catholic priest comes up and speaks with me. He was in this town the previous year when his mother died, so he feels a connection with this place and has promised to himself to return here each year. We speak about what is wrong with the world. I tell him again my sense about Greece being buried, and if we don't reignite values that enliven or respect and love in a new light, then civilization as we know it will remain in the doldrums calling in its end. He is fascinated by the idea and has caught on to my focus on goodness in humankind. He tells me I am typically Indian. I don't know what he means by that, but I take it as a compliment and thank him. He thinks we might meet here again. I nod, but I also think that we may not.

A Lithuanian woman who works for the resort feels a resistance to me; it is peculiar but somewhat familiar. We are strangers. She wants to feel she's better than anyone. I tell her that people think I may be from Crete. She denies it hotly. When the French woman asks me if I am Greek, the Lithuanian insists that I am not. The French woman says that I look like the women in the frescoes. The Lithuanian is silenced. It is interesting to be spoken about in the third person while being present. Smiling, I leave them to discuss my foreign presence.

I turn my attention to another group of people whose names I don't remember. The evening is fleet-footed and strange. What unfinished business did we have? I don't know. Perhaps, just to say this and that, to tie up lose threads, the unwinding ball of silk lingers sifts sprinkled in the moon-shot waves.

After the guests leave, the family discuss plans for their resort, all in Greek of course. I then ask when I may leave, as I need to be driven back to Hersonissos. Nestor is not available and I do not see him again. The mother arranges for a driver; I leave at 10:30 p.m. This is my last night in Hersonissos.

I do not want to miss my *yaourti* for breakfast. Even though Timos, the night clerk at the hotel, has been obsessively peculiar—friendly, then not—the visit has been intriguing. Living is not always easy for these people who live on the mainland and come to the islands for work during the tourist season. This is how many people must make a living. And Timos, has come all the way from Thessaloniki to work the summer months in Cretan resorts; he does what he can to serve the guests. It may seem like a lovely life, but it must have its difficulties.

Dreams must come true for us to feel human. Does manifesting make us godlike? I am curious. He gets ready to tell me a story. I am wide-eyed and all ears.

Hunchback of Hersonissos...

Many years ago, maybe 40 or 50, they say, a man named Petro came to a village from mainland. He is tall, about 6' 2" and stately, but looked sad. He is married to Helen, who has such loud voice no one could speak when she opens her mouth. As a result, Petro himself grew shorrterr and shorrterr, until he really couldn't give up any more of his height. He lost his stature and was down by one whole foot. All because his wife was so loud!

In point of fact, her rising decibels make fruits fall from trees, windows rattle, and crawling insects scuttle away in panic. Some say that even snakes would suddenly coil up and remain in camouflage.

The falling of fruits may have been helpful to some farmers who did not have many hands to help pick the fruit. But, of course, if the fruit were too ripe, they would be damaged. So that would be a loss. And the rattling of the windows was never a good thing during the warr and during the time of the Turrkish occupation. Except maybe to alert people that she was near, so they could hide. Literally hide so they would not have to deal with her, a sometimes very sad Helen.

But the most horrific thing that happened— maybe not the most horrific, just one more horrific thing—was that her baby was born with his face looking to one side as though to cover his earrs. They named this boy Aftiavich. So he grew up, he starrted to bend down morre and morre.

In order to straighten him up, his grandmother tied a stick to his back. But even she could not help. She was completely at herr wits' end as to how to make herr daughterr soften up, come down several decibels. Her daughterr, Helen, was beautiful but had been born loud,

194

and nothing could help her any more. The mother – grandmother – realized she had been cursed for her infidelity (too many) when Helen was an embryo fighting for her life in the little womb. So they all had to live with this...this currse.

They could not return to theirr home village because they would have been booted out again. The only reason that this new village allowed them in was that Petro brought them good luck. When he arrived, there was rain, which had been in hiding for some seasons and the land had gone dry. For all his bad luck, he brought good luck to others. They tolerated his wife because they liked him. And his boy, poor boy...

So Aftiavich grew up in this small rocky village, his body harrdening in an awkward shape as rocks hardened under a scorching sun. His childhood was not always nice enough, for he was teased and taunted by the village children. Some called him ugly names; some sang silly songs around him. He learrned to hide within himself, become shy. But there was one child who was kind to Aftiavich and would pry him away from the crowd, and they would go and play in the forest, swim in the sea.

So he grew, slowly but surrely. His upper back bent slightly, some say he bent down because of his mother's loud voice that he would try to avoid. Others say he bent in order to hear his father better. His father was now 4' 6" or so. His mother remained a robust hearty almost six-foot-tall woman whose voice (oh god!) never calmed down, not even when they forced garrlic down her throat on every full moon. Had to hold her down with 2 oxen.

In the listening of the tale, I admit I may have missed something, for my mind wandered. I am endeared to the

195

dreamy Aftiavich, so I recreate as best as I can; story is in two merged styles—his and mostly mostly mine. Mine.

In time, Aftiavich's grandmother, all dressed in black, sat on a rocking chair in a quiet corner of the house. She would look with kind eyes at her grandson, praying with cross in her hand to change his fate somehow. As he grew into manhood, his hunchback did not look so bad, perhaps because he was a little bit tallerr. To compensate for his stature, he starrted to look up a little. This made his face, his chin jut out some, giving him like a dinosaur appearance, but he had a nice kind face. His eyes always looked at everyone with gentleness. He had developed an angelic frankness in his eyes as though he appreciated the world as it was.

If anyone looked at him, he'd always look back. He would flutterr his eyelashes and smile. He really wanted people to like him. He would smile at them even if they did not smile back. In some ways, he was very endearing. Of course, his friend had disappeared one day, and Aftiavich was left alone again. He was essentially lonely. His mother was too full with voice to be a real person; his father went about his business shut in his silence.

One day when he was 39—his earlier years were quite uneventful and maybe forgettable—a woman was kind enough to give him a job at her hotel. He was now the night concierge. His duties included serving breakfast, answering tourist's questions, and checking in people who arrived late.

He would sit by the large screen TV with the fan on. This was the only fan in the village for miles, it seemed. None of the guests had a fan in the room. The hotel did not provide any.

It was one of those nights of wild partying next door with loud music and people walking in and out of the hotel randomly. Aftiavich returned from a stroll with the guys and went inside the kitchen. He returned with a glass of water and made himself comfortable on a single-seat sofa. He turned on the television, his channel into another world of the imagination.

After some time, he became bleary-eyed watching some game show with curvy women in bikinis standing on glass platforms over pools. Lights dazzled him. He chuckled from time to time. He wasn't sure whether the women were women or whether the women were fish...or maybe even flying fish. Do mermaids sing? Do they fly? Were the fish women?

A real woman entered the reception area. She was soaking wet, having just come out of the navy dark sea. She stood looking around her. She wanted the key to her room. She was lovely, svelte with dark brown hair curling around her face. But it was her almond eyes that grabbed Aftiavich. He couldn't get his eyes off her eyes, her face. She must be around 35 or 29 or 42. Well, he couldn't tell and it didn't matter. He knew this person had been sent herre for him. This angel was his to have and to hold. Till death. He was so sure of it that he reached out as if to stroke her, but she was at the other end of the room. Instead, he knocked over his glass of juice.

Embarrassed, he got up and slouched over to the woman waiting by the counter wanting her key so she could go up to her room. He smiled his sweet sweet smile, fished out the key from the basket, gave it to her and reached out to stroke her arm as a gesture of comfort. She thanked him for the key, smiled and left in the rickety elevator without lights.

Aftiavich stood staring after her, his eyes dreamy and wistful, his arm reaching out as if to touch a star hanging down from the sky. A flash of light from outside circling around suddenly fell on him like a spotlight and brought him out of reverie. He returned to the television, to another world of dreams.

She stayed at the hotel for one week. He waited eagerly for her to come back each evening. He waited to serrve her breakfast in the mornings. It was his job to set out the breakfast. He made it a point to pour her coffee or tea, whatever she wanted. He tried to speak with her. He made small conversation; he smiled ingratiatingly. "Whateverrr you want, ask me. Okay?" he said to her as she got up to leave. She nodded, thanked him and would leave the room. He would stand staring at her departing figure, his face sticking out of his neck in longing.

He'd come earlier than required for his duty. He brought her a lovely yellow fully blossoming chrysanthemum, but by the time she returned from her swim, it had wilted. He was sad and sat nursing the flower in front of the television. She did not come this evening. He waited. He went up and took her the fan he used and left it outside her door, tying it to her door handle so no one else would swipe it.

Finally, she arrived. But she was not alone. Her friend had arrived from France to join her. He looked at her as though she had betrayed a secret, yet he looked right through the man—the man did not exist. He forgave the woman and said, "This misterria...it betterrrr...you use. Okay?" And he stroked her arm as he turned to leave.

The next morning as usual he waited for her to come down for breakfast. She came down in a yellow robe flowing behind her like a queenly train.

198

Here he was in a smart pair of pants and new shirt, pressed to perfection as if he were going on the date of his life. She noticed and commented on his outfit. He was beyond joy. He knew she was his already. While he was serving the guests their morning teas and coffees, he heard a loud voice down the street. This was disaster approaching. Instinctively, he bent down even more. She noticed it and asked if he were okay. He said, "Yes...I okay...and you?... yes, okay?"

She nodded yes and turned to her breakfast. "Oh, thanks for the fan, Aftia...uh..vich," she said.

"Yes...Aftia...yes, good err...Fan? No problem...no problem," he smiled his angelic smile even as the voice outside grew louder and louder and he bent down even more. "I go now...see you tomorrow...no tonight." He winked at her and nodding left the room with a slight wave of this hand.

She picked up her coffee cup and saw there a note. It was from Aftiavich. She looked up but he had left; she saw his humble body shuffling away on the street towards the loud voice. Truly, she felt a little sorry for him—he had been so kind—but she also felt a mild perturbed. She did not like that loud noise that called him away, for really he was nice.

She went about her day with her friend. Both loved to carouse through shops and swim. But today they drove out of the village to hike in the mountains and maybe have dinner in Agios Nikolaos.

Aftiavich's day was the same. Some rest and then running errands for his mother, whose beautiful face had become pointed and sharp, her voice as loud, perhaps a little rasping. Truly, he was sick of it all. But his angel had arrived and he found his spirits lifting, lifting, lifting...

He began to hear music in the grasses. Flowers by the wayside looked more sweetly alive than ever before. In fact, he noticed them maybe for the first time. Just as he was getting feverish in his reverie, his mother began her screaming again. Try hard as he might, this was one sound he could not transform into music. Sadly so, because... (well, you'll see).

So, he went to work as usual, but his angel was not there. In fact, he laid out a bouquet of the singing alive flowers he'd picked from the wayside beside her door. He made the front counter neat and tidy and placed her key in the basket very nicely and settled in front of the television as was his routine. The clock turned on the hour, the party next door carried on as usual, loud and self-absorbed. She did not come.

He must have fallen asleep—it was early in the morning. She came back with her friend; they picked up the key and went upstairs. She was tired and a wee bit tipsy. From the corner of her eye, she saw him nodding on his chest and smiled as she remembered his rushing gush of affection. The note was safe in her bag. It was a nice keepsake of her visit. She truly wished him well.

Aftiavich woke up to perform his morning rites of serving breakfast. He looked up at the stairs from time to time. Breakfast eaters came down singly or in twos and threes and left. She did not come. He was crestfallen and began to look ill as he left for home.

By midday, the angel came down with her bags and her boyfriend and they checked out. They were all set to leave when she came back to the foyer and went to the counter to Thespina, the day receptionist.

200

*"Thespina, this box is for Aftia...please give it to him,"
and she left.*

*When Aftiavich arrived that night, he found the
small box. In it was a beautiful crystal angel, small and
rose tinted. With wings. He held it tightly in his hands,
then, pocketing it, he went about his work dully.*

*After some days, people noticed that he looked
very pale, even ashen. Thespina's mother was concerned
and insisted he take some days off. Helen screamed
down the neighborhood shouting curses at anyone who
might have looked at or tried to steal her son from her.*

*Aftiavich could take it no longer. He shut his
ears tight and let out a long howl. He would not stop. He
could not. People tried to hold him and stuff his mouth,
but there was suddenly so much strength in him that no
one dared come near.*

He continued to howl—loud and strong.

*People said that if he had bawled loudly as a
baby perhaps he would have had the strength to handle
anything and anyone—of course, they meant his
mother—but be that as it may, he had been a puny,
quiet sickly child. Now, they wondered what had
become of him. Or what had taken over him. They
retreated in the face of a stiff challenge from Aftiavich.
No one dared go near. They stayed away.*

*His mother became a little quiet. In their house,
the grandmother, almost sullen and turned to stone
over the years, was finally able to smile. And his father
looked up and saw the sun squarely in the face after
many years. Aftiavich left the house early in the
morning clutching his angel to his heart.*

He went to the sea to the part where he used to play as a child. Not many people went to this spot, for getting there was a challenge rather perilous. He had gone there with his little friend, his only friend who had stood by him as his back slowly hunched over.

He found himself a nice blue rubber float. He found a large pair of goggles and put them on. He undressed and his curved back shone in the morning sun. He lay down on the float and went out to sea, comfortably ensconced on the float now moving gently with the rhythm of the waves.

He swam amid angels who had not only wings but also mermaid's tails. They floated this way and that way, taking him along with them. All pain was forgotten. All he saw were beautiful hands caressing him and....

Ah! Here is his angel, herself, in flowing yellow moving her lips, smiling. She is saying something to him. He smiles. He flutters his eyes and winks at her. He reaches out to caress her bare wet shoulder.

He knows now that she had never left, that he had imagined it. He knows now what he had known all along, that she was and is his. He knows this as he knows that the fish never stop smiling, that the birds never stop singing to him, and that the angels of the waters take him home.

In his home, he never stops dreaming.

That was the one night when Aftiavich traveled away into his dreams that the mosquitoes invaded the hotel, the land and the fan; the only fan in the hotel refused to turn again.

Rising of Last Moments

My last day in Crete is a Sunday. Pepe Glavan, who has been my travel coordinator here, picks me up for a drive through the villages with Knossos as the final destination. We find almost all attractions are closed, except, of course, Knossos. The busyness of other days leaves me less curious for details. The noise of the heat, the glare of the sun, the stream of tourists has become intense and seem to encompass all, even saturate the walls of ruins. I wish to meander with ease and float among images, perceptions, posed structures, wherein I can hear the inner music of things. The earth sings a rich song with many layers as heat meets the dust, the crinkling of plants holding on for sustenance, and the sky passing by.

Driving through small villages is a lesson in Cretan culture even though they look deserted in this hot weather. Arriving at Knossos becomes a tender journey. On the way, we stop for directions, and a group of women sitting by the side of the road are excited to speak with us. They invite us to eat with them, but Pepe is on a schedule. The church nearby is closed, they say, so we continue our drive. In Greek, the word for "yes" is "nay"; this creates amusement and confusion between us, especially when we speak to clarify the next step on our journey. That is when I realize I am saying "yes" when I mean "no" and why he keeps doing the opposite of what I request.

Arriving at the Minoan capital, Knossos, moves me to stillness. To be in this place inhabited for thousands of years beginning with a Neolithic settlement is memorable in itself. This place is grand and woven with intricate complexities that make our modern accomplishments less than groundbreaking. I am not sure if this one feature existed then, but when we arrive at these tourist Meccas, we are greeted by shoppers and vendors. Indeed, the mercantile element makes the world go around and crazy. Here are shops selling icons before we can get to the main attraction—the palace and grounds designed by architect and inventor Daedalus, imprisoned here

203

so he would not create another magnificent work of art for a patron anywhere else.

Such things have happened in other parts of the world. It is said that after the Taj Mahal was built in Agra, India, the Mughal Emperor Shah Jahan had the artisans' hands chopped off so they would not build another monument of such exquisite beauty. This act of hubris was so severe that the emperor was himself imprisoned by his son in bid to usurp power and was not allowed to look at the luminous ode he had created for his beloved. Both he and Mumtaz Mahal lie buried in this beauteous mausoleum, one of many built just to revere the glorious dead.

In a rush to explore, I soon move into the line of people walking to the entrance to reconstruct, if possible, what transpired here thousands of years ago. Administrative center of the Minoan culture, the palace itself is designed with great attention to detail: the interconnected chambers, columns that support the portico of the halls, delicately painted frescoes that re-tell myths painted for the residents of old Knossos. But a famous story that remains with most of us is the story of the labyrinth where ruled the Minotaur.

A version of the story tells us that King Aegeus lost a war to King Minos and was required to send seven boys and seven girls to the Minotaur, who would devour them. Is it possible that this tale suggests an astronomical shift in the turning of the skies to reveal new patterns? Theseus was the hero chosen to slay the Minotaur, thus astrologically marking the change from Taurus to Aries. King Aegeus passes on, and, Theseus not only frees Crete of the Minotaur, but also becomes king of Athens.

Here, also is the story of Ariadne, about whom I was made curious in Thessaloniki. Daughter of King Minos, she gives Theseus the ball of thread to find his way out of the labyrinth after he has slain the Minotaur, the very labyrinth built by the master Daedalus. They are to wed, but don't. He leaves the island without her. She is bereft by this loss, but in the end, she weds Dionysus, god of wine and roses.

I am curious to see this labyrinth, but we do not have access to it, or it was destroyed in earlier years. Perhaps, we are not privy to the places of subconscious dramas of the old culture, except by conjecture. Pattern of a symbolic journey in Celtic lore, the labyrinth could very well be this subconscious that dramatizes psyche's darkness; in this case, the unruly killings as a mark of victory. The labyrinth also promises a journey into the inner sanctum, where the gold resides.

Here are physical boundaries, and in truth, we have always access to our sub-conscious, non-conscious and un-conscious. What if we tuned in to our hidden motivations and dramas, to the labyrinths that reside in us, would be learn to make better choices? What a springing spiral we are as we trace our clarity by dipping into the abyss and emerge repeatedly into a better self-identification. Imagine a vertical line with a spiral emerging from its base and moving on up around and around this line with each consecutive state becoming more refined as it travels upwards where light pours through awaking the roots down below. They stir and silk threads unwind as we travel out of this to the light's beckoning.

I am pulled out of trance as Pepe calls out to tell me we should hurry. But I must take a look at the tall beautiful earthen jars, which have always intrigued me. I am a vessel who has not explored this part of me yet.

Before this trip, I had seen in a dream a pot with three-petaled lips for a rim, so I wish to find one like that; I realize this was unique to my dream. I had painted it. Now I take pictures of other pots, large and pendulous, as they stand lovingly forgotten beside the walls in neat rows. Terracotta pots bring me home...I recall Kabir's verse:

Maati kahe kumhar se/ Tu kya raunde moye/ Ik din aisa aavega/ Main raundoongi toye.

These lines translate to: Clay says to the potter/ you knead me to the dust/ one day like this will come/ when I will do the same to you.

As I walk from room to room, I see unfolding before me exquisite frescos of dolphins, bulls, and the women of Crete with long flowing curls. I am one of them, I am so sure now. I remember what the tour guide who had insisted Ariadne and I share a likeness, Elpida, had said in Saloniki as well as the Cretan woman on the boat: they were convinced I am from this land. I smile at this thought of having to see myself wherever I travel as though I have been to these places in other life times. I probably have as I feel an affinity in many parts of the world.

I am not sure how much historical detail I can grasp at this point. It seems really that such information is easier to absorb in silent reading, not touring. When there is time and space. Now I allow myself to be a tourist on the go; this is one way to see the world. We come to the ruins for visual and vivid impressions. To imagine what was and what could have been—to see in our mind's eye early agrarian times when we revered nature and lived with her rhythms.

After a few carefully chosen angels for photographs and feeling sated by this, we decide it is enough. The lunch at the local *taverna* across the street is welcome, even though it is the same as the delicious meal last time: *xorta, gemista*, salad. I eat everything that we order, realizing only after I start eating how terribly hungry I have been. The heat can disguise hunger—so can fatigue.

We drive from village to village on little narrow lanes that challenge our driving cars. Somehow, we always find a way out of tight spaces, not once grazing a car or being grazed by one. Smart cars work here, but not in a big city with big vehicles speeding around one...!

House of Kazantzakis

Eventually, we get to Mirto where Nikos Kazantzakis lived. Born in Irakleio, he lived here in Mirto, the birthplace of his father. The home he lived and grew up in was developed by his friend into a museum for the work that Kazantzakis accomplished in his lifetime.

Although the museum is humble, it offers many fine details and notes, handwritten documents, old photographs of the family of the renowned writer who brought greater fame to this island. I feel a strange thrill as I walk into this sleeping museum, which the caretaker opens especially for us.

These last few days, his autobiographical novel *Report to Greco* (1965) has been my companion. I bought the book at a vendor in Hersonissos and have carried this little paperback everywhere with me, reading snatches when I could. Born on Cretan soil with some Turkish influence, Kazantzakis blends characters as he sees himself in many of them, including the artist, El Greco. A rich fabric of moral longings and juxtapositions, artistic explorations and re-creations of self, *Report to Greco* must feel like a willing surrender or a profound ironic confessional, but it is much more.

It is truly a layered exploration into what it means to be a man with various excesses and a desire for that which is transitory and that which endures: the fullness and nihilism of love; the longing for it and freedom from it; the search for the space of dying into self; the desire to know what makes art; the purpose of all journeys; the love for land and a moral imperative to protect its pristine beauty, while destruction rages rampantly across the canvas of the mind and the heart. In all this, a man breaks, a man creates, a man becomes.

Even as I re-enter these spaces in recollection, I find I must extricate myself from these memories and meanderings so that I can stand whole here present with what I am doing now. Getting lost in another's story can be all consuming and not constructive, but glimpses offer answers to enduring questions. Now the familiar melody of Zorba the Greek wends its way to remind me that it is always dance that frees.

As we leave the museum and its environs, I notice that even the trash cans in the village proudly carry Kazantzakis' name. He is memory of mythic stature.

We return to Hersonissos at around 4 p.m. In a reflective frame of mind, I rest for a while in my stark room buzzing with mosquitoes. Shortly thereafter, I pack and go to the Majestic for tea and also to write. This final touch feels important and helps me to conclude a visit that has been hard but also interesting. Perhaps it is easier to travel with company: even angels, with wings or without, wish to hold hands sometimes.

I have very much enjoyed the goodness of Zabena, the German waitress at the Majestic—she's a single German woman who has left a devastating and unhappy marriage. Her young daughter stays with the grandmother in Germany. Zabena is excited to know more about India; she wishes to go there. She says a few times to me that she has always been drawn to shops with Indian things, colors, designs, and religious icons. I feel she will go when she feels stable and knows better her purpose. Now she is not ready, even though she is excited by the image of India and what my presence and motherland represent to her. She has indeed been kind to me, helped me battle mosquitoes with mosquito-repellant coil like those we use in India.

Laughing, Zabena tells me she has taught her boss a thing or two about time. I complain to her that these guys commit to one time, but show up one, maybe, even two hours later than the time they schedule. She twinkles and says she had the same problem with her boss. Finally, one day she told him, if he is more than ten minutes late for an appointment with her, she won't wait up for him. She keeps her word, and he has gotten the message. I take her happy picture. She says she is generally happy and also very easy going, but when someone gets her mad, they'd better watch out. I believe her. This is my goodbye tea.

Finally, Pepe Glavan shows up with a wildly content smile and drives me to the harbor at Irakleio. I board the Festos Palace, a tiny city with a pool, shops, many restaurants, play areas, a tennis court. This is a humongous ship—a labyrinth of commerce. I walk from section to section in search of a seat that would satisfy my need of being away from smokers and of relative quiet. I find a seat that is somewhat comfortable, but the noise and constant traffic grate on me. In a fit of discomfiture, I carry my bag and look for another place.

Feeling a little like a fool, I look around in nearby spaces aware of wandering eyes on me. It does not matter what the signs say, people will smoke anyway. I find another seat, but it is bumpy, dilapidated, and a bit torn. My longing eyes note the other seat at the far end of this space is now taken. I wished now I had kept the old one. One cannot escape cigarette fumes. Otherwise, I think I have done very well in Greece.

Soon I am to find out, Greece has brought me back my interest in food. I am eating better for having enjoyed foods cooked in pure olive oil and lemon. Vara was right: in Greece you must love to eat.

I am finally at sea moving away from Crete and returning to Athens. I am wondering how I am changed thus far. I feel a bit sad for not being able to visit Samaria Gorge or Chania, which would have offered a quieter repast as photos have suggested. Sometimes photographs inspire a new adventure.

And destiny? Angelopoulos. Of course. Even as I think about him, I see a hand as big as a five-storey building move across the horizon. This is the opening scene from his film, *Ulysses' Gaze.*

How far shall we go before we find ourselves in our own hearts? How far must I wander? Losing oneself is a step to finding oneself deep within.

Beginning to long for silence I am
and for space –
space within – drops of nectar
golden-rose
in heart chamber
contained amid five petals
solace

of embrace.

"It is equally wrong to speed a guest who does not want to go, and to keep one back who is eager. You ought to make welcome the present guest, and send forth the one who wishes to go."

~ Homer

Chapter 10 ~ Twists and Turns of Being in Athens

Safely returned to Athens, I begin to feel ready to return home to Los Angeles. The journey to the islands has left me somewhat tired, and I am uncertain of what more I can do. Unease prickles through my heart; I feel homesick. I try to change the departure date to leave sooner, but all flights are booked. It is nearly impossible. Concerned at how I am feeling, Selene, in her kindness, invites me to go to Tinos with her friend Milos, who knows the place well. I agree despite my apprehension about another visit out of the capital.

We walk into and out of worlds. The strange becomes familiar and then again strange: one can come only this close and no more. I had asked for Greece to free me from myself. Now I wish for ease, grace, comfort of cool gardens, and the familiarity of home, without the sordidness of dark places. Taking a journey must be a pleasure, not always a lesson. The purpose of a journey changes at every step. When you take one step towards your destination, does the destination take a step towards you? Or does it pull you away from one thing to something else? Is Destiny fixed or fluid or both?

Why are we so obsessed with purpose? It is a preoccupation in these modern times. But simply to be free is this; then it is not purpose but a state of being we must ask for. And have it by being aware of it. By simplifying our lives.

Meropi, the Albanian, walks into the kitchen where I am making tea, invites me to visit the Plaka; perhaps, we can buy souvenirs like the blue eye to ward off dark forces, then eat with Nico, Meropi's fiance, and his friend. But after a long trip to Crete and Santorini, I feel squished by trucks of time, fatigue and lack of desire to go anywhere just to go somewhere. Especially to buy trinkets.

But plans are made for Tinos and Milos arrives the next day to take me to his mother's house. Before leaving, I help Thaleia choose her clothes and jewelry for a wedding she will attend on Sunday night. She picks the gaudy flashier jewelry and baulks at my choice of the elegant quiet pieces that match her dress. She is so full of glee that I have to smile. I compliment her; she smiles like morning glory.

We reach Glyfada late. Milos assures me it is okay and Selene has prepared the guest bed for me in the neighboring studio. I settle in for a short while, but when the air conditioning stops, I wake up with a shock. The stillness weighs heavily in the room; I doze in the in-between spaces.

I want to call home, listen to Indian tones, familial voices.

When I finally wake up, it is close to 6 a.m. I get ready for another adventure to this well-known Cycladic island.

We buy tickets at Piraeaus and run in between slips to find our monster of the seas. With a mad scramble up, we soon find two seats in the non-smoking area. I sit near a short older woman who is crocheting a skirt for a grandchild. I watch her keenness as the piece takes form. Suddenly, the loose threads roll off the spool and she pulls out more of it. The thread is soft, white, silky. I change places with Milos so I can help the woman. She smiles a "no, thanks, it is alright." But I insist and help her unravel the skeins from the floor. Once it is all untangled, I gesture that I will hold the threads around my two fore arms, so she can unwind it from there and wrap it around a made-up spool into a ball. This silent collaboration is nice. It is something I did as a child when Mimi, my grandmother, prepared wool for knitting.

We manage to unravel most of it and then wind it round into a ball again. It feels like finding a way out of the labyrinth of my mind, of the cosmos and into a labyrinth of the heart. It brings me to stillness; this stillness excites me into reverie and restfulness. I am on another journey. Already.

In silence we find our peace and connectedness. There is harmony in these moments; the *sutra*, the thread, connects

212

us all. The *Sutra* in its winding weaves of cosmic grammar holds worlds together—like the Word that was and is. Sutras tell of the threads of the heart, which like a trillion cosmic cords keeps us inter-connected. So how can we ever be lost?

Is not the thread an ancient metaphor that after connecting all dots, twists, turns, it brings us out of stupor into our eternal relatedness? Shiva-Shakti sutras, indeed, are the cosmic cords that reverberate through all our being: accompanying this is a process of awakening so priceless that all dialectics after being observed become absorbed in the dance of dissolution; this dissolution has to be complete in order for us, or an adept, to become beyond any and all dissatisfactions, theories, amalgamations, discussions, digressions, arguments, *vaad-vivaad (dialogue and debate)*, to become that utter bliss, so as unique expression be in complete service for the greater good. Boddhisattva!

I am not an adept—I am a seeker with a wee gift for some poetry, a kind of a threaded garment, which I hope illumines.

The thread goes through the eye of a needle. Threads hold garments together: our glances are threads of anger, joy, sorrow, and of loving. The singular thread ought to always be of bliss. Even as the boat churns in the wild blue-shaded sea, I think of inequities of life, not as sparking a longing but a sense of being less than. Longing springs from desire for that which is greater that within resides.

Every now and then, Milos looks at us two women wrapped in our shared space and urges me to "Leave it...let it go now." It feels as though he is partly amused, partly confused with this new camaraderie between women. I feel his lost-ness, but he has other interests, and I realize he is dogged by lack of purpose. But I am enjoying my time as I recall how my grandmother would make us sit with our arms bent at the elbows with the wool around our wrists...she would then wind it into balls so she could knit cardigans for us kids. This is familiar. This is old. Those were days that cannot return.

He takes off to the promenade, somewhat sulking, then returns with the same words, "Leave it...leave it." But, "I am having fun doing this." I truly am. The special quiet place we share is nice—this woman and I. She is making a skirt for her granddaughter. I take some pictures of her. Milos feels left out, I understand. I have gotten involved with what women did that created community. In a few minutes, I "leave it" in a place where the woman does not need me anymore. I wonder how we can create such community again in our diverse societies where we do not sit and shell peas any more. Do our teens know this term, "shelling peas"?

We walk on the deck and look at waves driving along the sides of the big boat. We are reaching Sira. We look for new seats but someone already has marked these for themselves. We take seats near the old ones. I snooze. When I wake up, I see the woman has left. No goodbye—and a little tug in me—then satisfaction for having helped her. We find seats by the porthole where we spend the remainder of the journey watching waves go by.

Language is an oddity. How do waves go by when no wave is a singularly formulated entity but a purely fluid process, the way the cosmos inter/intra is—even perhaps, the way we inter-are: both change and force of change, both crest and bottom of crest, both love and not-love. The way sand dunes undulate, so do waves; particles of water move faster than those of sand. The way pleasure can become pain and return as pleasure. The way we fall and rise in love. The way we swallow food in wave motion. The way we reach our destination...and learn end from beginnings until we cannot tell the difference. We look at the continuity of things, for our experience of such movements is real.

We arrive in Tinos.

The heat in Tinos is like blasts from a huge oven. We get information on boat departures to mainland before taking the bus to the village of Falatados. On the way, Milos inspires me with information on local architecture. He points out the houses that are built to accommodate pigeons, "so many pigeons." I wonder about the strange relationship that people have with pigeons on this island. There is something mysterious about it, and I want to know it more. I am moved by it, but sadly we have just one day here. My traveling companion thinks my sudden sentimentality to be strange—I wonder at my imagination. How can I explain such concepts to one who has little experience of the world outside of his environs? Better to keep to surface of things, while enjoying nuggets of wisdom that surprise me; he is kind.

We go to the *taverna*, which is run by friends of his family. I am to stay with Dora, a seventy-nine-year-old lady, on the floor above the *taverna*. Dora is tall, slender, with a strict and proper mien. This would be a quiet time, as I speak no Greek and she speaks no English. She shows me to my room. I leave my bags; we walk up the slope another seven to eight minutes to his great-aunt's house.

Zakharoula is an elegantly poised homely woman. She is Mama Melpo's near cousin, which makes her my host, Athanas's distant aunt. She is in the house with her daughter-in-law, a winsome Zena; grandchildren, Tia and Zoe the twins and Calix the infant boy; Zena's father prepares whitewash for the walls. Both Zakharoula and Zena would like us to stay to eat with them instead of at the *taverna*. Tia and Zoe act up for me. Tia shyly hides, yells, laughs to call my attention. I play for a while. We do not speak a common language other than the codes of hide and seek.

In the meanwhile, Zena sets the table and calls us to stop the running around. We are served salad, green beans, bread, beans with potatoes, pasta with meat. We feast heartily on this rich repast. I notice Zakharoula looking at me keenly from where she sits. I smile. In this environment, I feel something different about Milos' energy; he is suddenly more grown up, mature, and responsible. People change in the company of different people.

Zena won't let me help pick up stuff from the table, not even the bread. The space is small. I find some knitting and start to knit. Zena is knitting a sweater for herself. Milos laughs and shakes his head and says, "Leave it...why?" and so on. I carry on knitting; I am actually enjoying it. He tells them the story of the woman on the boat with the fallen skeins of thread. I smile a little remembering the ball of silk thread. It's a wonderful time.

A full belly and rhythm of knitting make me drowsy. I feel obsessed with the knitting as it takes on more meanings: the weaving of cosmos, of thoughts, of making something whole. I remember the fable about the woman who would weave stories of the universe even as her dog would unravel it. This continued into her old age, but she would never finish it, for were she to add the last stitch, the world would come to an end. The dog was the savior—!

Weaving is the fabrication of the universe. The word "fabric" derives from the Latin *"fabrere,"* "to weave." The weave is endless, a matrix of galaxies, wherein we are holograms of light. How can I not see this, as so much light dances around us unceasing, relentlessly continuing all re-creation? Yes, by now I am sitting outside on the steps in the shy shade of the wall.

To continue a connection, Zakharoula comes out and tells me to rest, brings me a pillowcase and bed sheet. She insists, but I say I am okay. She's feeling protective towards me. I watch her from the corner of my eye. Before Milos goes for his shower, she comes up to him and whispers in his ears. I knit, sensing she is making queries. He smiles; I don't know if it is *apropos* to use the words "coy" or "demure" for a male; perhaps, the knitting is making me feel demure, but it is a good thing, a girly thing. How we'd rebel when mother wanted us to knit and sew, we who would look down at girly things...! I knit those moments into the sweater, which is a blend of many colors...pink, green, brown, gold...a pattern emerges.

After his shower, Milos walks me to my room atop the *taverna*. Milos asks if I don't mind being left to myself. I insist I need it. He will come later in the evening after he has taken care of his business. This alone time I need so badly. We've been on the move since 7 a.m. and I haven't slept more than two hours.

My nap drowns me into deep slumber. When Milos arrives, I am in a stupor, half awake—some of it is heat-induced. He waits, talks with the lady of the house. I laze for a few moments, wondering how to get the beads out of my eyes.

216

Gradually, I rise, stretch, and get myself washed and ready. We leave for the *taverna* downstairs.

We sip mountain sage tea while we wait for Zena to come down to take us to Volax, a village built to integrate natural features of the rocky land. Large rocks make walls for homes. Other rooms are added on connecting room to room. One house comes out of another house, or a cave out of a cave.

Our contemporary apartment buildings are boxes next to boxes, without the appeal of roundness or forms resembling nature. But this little village of Volax, built with its local materials, walls of mountain and stone, is magical. I am impressed with this concept of interlocked houses, and I wonder which of the famous architects have visited this small island of so much richness. This old village already has the right idea. The place charms and delights me with its simplicity, rusticity, and rhythms.

We visit the small museum that displays a traditional home in the village as well as the traditional dress of the people of the village or the island. Volax also has its own small theater built around rocks, which are part of the seating arena; in America those rocks would have been hewn away to make more seats, which equal more money. Here we see integration; this is poetic. Angelopoulos, the filmmaker, would approve. The audience is part of nature is part of theatrical action is life.... Is this an aspect of the real Greece as he defines it? He and I both know Greece is buried. I feel warmed at this thought of mutuality between both our perceptions.

We drive back to Falatados in the dark. At this time, the island's mysterious rugged beauty is savagely illumined. It awakens something in me: a longing to own one of these interwoven homes, a home away from home. My imagination wanders beyond the Aegean Sea and back to its rushing waves, even as the small rusty car wends its way over and around curving mountain road. High up there, it feels as though the road is part of a road in the sky.

Let us fly
beyond moon landings behind

217

where crickets dwell in wild symphony

Let us sing songs
to nourish earth's riches
big rock where lovers pray
for their nuptials

Let us call on the custodians
to awake and rub the ache
away from Gaia's skins
        So conserve inspire love.

The rock eludes the wary
Fears keep lovers apart
far from a cathedral of dreams

The arched sky houses
all our dreams...passion to endure
        ache of all Love!

Zena, the kids, Milos and I decide to first eat at the *taverna* and then go into Tinos, which disappears in the night sky; we return to the home *taverna* for a dinner of *gemista, xorta* and meat patties. Surrounded by satin night spreading all around us, we enjoy the meal amid chatter in various world languages. At another table is a group of people from Holland celebrating a birthday. At another is Brigitte, an art historian who works at a museum in Frankfurt and her partner, also an art historian and a teacher. Her open graciousness is a fine counterpoint to his reticence. We have a delightful conversation over watermelon and *kafé nero*; she explains her desire to merge in the silent beauty of Tinos, even though she loves her work as an historian. We are all in search of something other than what we have.

We talk about travels, art, about the pigeon houses on Tinos. We share our fantasies with camaraderie and glee. I recall how as a child of eleven, I had imagined a big blue snake entering the bathroom where I was about to take a shower.

But suddenly I had become frightened because the snake had become real. It had filled the room with itself and wouldn't stop filling it even more. I had closed my eyes and showered and then run out to see if it was still coming into the room— my imaginary creation had become all too big for me.

We are each a story within a story within a story, *ad infinitum*. At the core under all these stories are eyes that see and remember. In the moment, it is Milos, for beyond his eyes are his smile, but much uncertainty. I imagine that beyond the smile there must be light. I imagine anyone who smiles with ease must have light dancing inside; I am good at deluding myself. I am so excited that we could make a trip to the big rock, that it drives Milos to shake his head and protest. "We'll see." The couple laughs at my enthusiasm and at Milos' confusion at my excitement over things. He is a young one assigned to show me around. And I am pushing on his boundaries, maybe even mine.

There is a call for *kafé nero*. I tell Brigitte about Stavros reading my coffee dregs. She is intrigued. Her guy gets us some coffee. The blackness of the coffee against a sky studded with diamonds invites Brigitte and me to exchange e-mail addresses. I tell her that Stavros had said this would happen. She smiles. Perhaps I will hear from her sometime; she has a gentle face. I never do. Chance meetings happen to remind us of something or to suggest a new direction or to share an insight that makes the moment beautiful.

We walk to Zakharoula's home and make ourselves comfortable by the steps waiting for the family to return from the town. The stars look smaller than the ones over Cozumel, Mexico, but, of course, they are the same stars. It's lovely lying stretched on a ledge of a home in a typical Cycladic village looking up at the night sky. Milos sits on a chair beside me, chattering away. I forget what he says—the night sky is so remarkable: She invites me to wonder... just to wonder.

Does purpose itself purposively fulfill life's destiny and self-knowledge into wholeness through *smriti*— remembering All That One Is—immanent god-light, and what one is not? Does desire stir purpose into action? The desire to write a story or build a home or business moves us to clarify and attain our purpose.

Life's ultimate destiny continually confronts us by revealing transcendent moments—every little thing we do points to that river, which feeds tributaries, which go into the great big beyond sea. Desire and purpose are the intra-connected network that drive us; the end of the big journey is inevitable. With laughter and tears, triumphs and losses, Swift's Lestrygonians would insist.

I ask Milos what is his desire and purpose; he has no answer. He laughs uncertainly, wondering why I ask serious questions.

Star from afar gazes
with million twinkling eyes
my arms open wide

I am a point
facing all directions:
Stillness Breath Wonder

Shall I leave the world
Or be that...destiny –
the love that weaves?

His relatives arrive soon thereafter. Zena comes up and tugs my chin—I feel like a kid when she does that—and asks how our visit was to Tinos. We did not go, Milos tells her, but we sat and socialized with the German couple. I am slightly amused by Zena.

We stay a little longer and chat with everyone. The sidewalls have been painted. I had wanted to help with this, but it's been done. Earlier I was too drowsy. Milos tells them I feel disappointed I did not lend a hand. The old man looks at me and asks if I like it all. I say, "yes." Or, perhaps, I nod. They smile. Milos gets up and plays with Zoe; how like a child he is

220

with the child, but with a sense of responsibility. We are all childlike in our finest moments.

I think of children yet to be born. How will they retain this playful innocence and teach the adults how to teach them!? I feel strongly that we must allow ourselves to be guided by our children on how to parent them; I feel that our parents lost out with social strictures that even they could not help themselves. It is time for a new dialogue between parents and their children, even adult children who must take charge and choose new direction.

We leave to walk through the village. It is past midnight. Mosquitoes are having a wild time gregariously buzzing around busily alighting on unsuspecting human beings. We walk past what was Melpo's house and out to where some people park their cars. I stand mesmerized by the stars, hearing them sing. It is so lovely the way night sounds tender as the light that comes streaming down the dark sky meets the song of cicadas. We continue our walk along trails between these Cycladic homes nestled against each other.

Milos then suggests we walk back. *Ney ney* I am only a wee disappointed; this place is so magical that the child in me wants to count the stars—I have loved Van Gogh's *Starry Night,* its vastness so charming. But this one is real. The only other time I remember a sky splattered with stars was on my visit to Cozumel in Mexico. Such magic it was you could stand on tiptoe and touch a star. We sit on a wall and share shoulder rubs. I am surprised he has strong hands. Should I have asked for a backrub after the swimming at the beach in Athens some days ago? I am cautious as I remember...

After a long swim near Glyfada, we had lain on the beach on two large manganese blue towels. I was on my belly—*kilitza*—and I had asked him to put rocks on my back. He had laughed and wondered what people would think. I didn't care, I said. So he placed rocks on my back. I breathed more easily. The earth had calmed my fatigue and grounded me. When I felt rested with the rocks, I offered to do the same for Milos. He hesitated and then allowed me. So I placed rocks on his back. This was for him a strange and exotic thing, a pushing of boundaries.

In this playfulness, I learned the power of rock therapy. It's solidifying and grounding to have weight placed on the body, which must still feel light and quick to move. It must feel safe and right. I promised myself a hot stone massage when I am back in Los Angeles.

Here on the stone walkway in Falatados, village of rock, lava, and cement, we fight mosquitoes, big buzzing creatures, invading our perceptions and enjoyment of stars twinkling in the night past midnight. It feels like being back in college in India, when we could be disobedient and take late walks, smoke cigarettes, and drink over philosophy and romance: freely wondering about the expansive Universe, the expectation of all things grand and wonderful, visions of saving the world from fraudulent practices, of eradicating hunger and poverty, of making the best films, writing the best poems, traveling to lands far and beyond...building a home, being special. I am startled by these thoughts. I feel impatient with myself. Such romances linger in the imagination, for it is after all an adventure with the soul.

Let imagination be a river that falls to the earth, makes her fecund and us too in new ways.

We continue our walk wrapped in night's textures. Each time I think we are going back to the *taverna*, he leads me to another part of the village, which is deserted at this time. We go past many homes woven into homes. How closely knit the communities had been at one time! Our sense of space has changed so much today.

Our dense urban spaces bread emotional trauma and violence. We have come to desire quietude and walks in nature. I wonder if this desire for quiet is cultural—people in warm cultures seem to need less personal space. I know how much I need private space but also resonant companionship.

The word "private" intrigues me. In Czech (and other East European languages) it is *"privat."* In Sanskrit, *"priya"* suggests "beloved one," or all that is dear to one. *Prideri* is precious one, the hero of the Welsh epic, *Mabinogion.* The root is *"priya"*—in order to establish private-ness, there must be at least two; thus, the sharing of common space is precious and inevitable. From relational private-ness, we get the business

222

entity, a private limited company. Felt states are bound by laws inherent in their way of being so we nurture what is within and what is without.

Why do we flaunt our loves, which are but private? We can share and integrate them, so we can enjoy them. It is not only a matter of social convention, but individual desire to keep sacred that which is private enclosed in an unspoken boundary, a circle, a space for loving, a home, a vista. Why cross the boundaries of promises? Why invite public scarring? I am speaking generally, not specifically about Falatados.

We walk through the grounds of the new church, whose bells ring on the hour without fail. Why in the middle of the night, we wonder? Suddenly, we find a flight of steps and climb up to a schoolhouse. It begins to feel almost Escherian. Milos points out another little church, in such a small space. We stop in different places and listen to the breathing of the village, its rhythm and pauses. Suddenly appears a tunnel beyond which is a quaint and novel house. I want to buy one here—I want a home everywhere.

We find yet another church. But it is late; the stars feel further away. I am yawning, a taste of boredom creeps in and I can't feign interest at this time; I simply desire to huddle in silence in the little cot offered me for the night. Silence in the churchyard feels strangely alien as I can hear the sky sing, but my feet ache. I am happy to return to my den for the time, a room in his great-aunt's house. The lady of the house has returned; it is past midnight. She invites him to stay for a while, but he declines. I say "*Kali nichta*" and turn in for the night. I watch him walk out of the living room into another dream.

The night is still remarkably beautiful, with stars softly nestling against the darkness. It is time to sleep, really to sleep despite the heat and mosquitoes. I think of stars, not so clearly visible in busy Los Angeles, where light dims the stars that recede into the distancing electric fog.

I tumble into bed, but the mosquitoes are a bother. I get up and ask Dora for some mosquito repellant. She first thinks I want an ashtray. Then she figures it out after my impromptu act dramatizing the impact of mosquitoes on me.

She plugs a repellant in my room. I smile; she smiles. We bid each other good night in Greek. I drift somewhere into arms of *oneiros* weaving another world....

How a Wing Readies for Flight

I awake very early and make my tea. It feels so good, warm and silky as it weaves its way through my body; I am in wonder. This place is lovely, and I wish we had more time to explore Tinos. After my tea, I lie down, still sleepy. It is now not even 7 a.m. I have had trouble sleeping; one needs patience in the heat. One has to make a mental effort not to feel it, but to carry on regardless and enjoy each moment as it unfolds.

Ants ply up and down the low wall of the terraced eating area of the *taverna*. I get up again and see that Dora is awake. She asks me to join her in the kitchen. She makes coffee; I make tea. We chat without understanding exactly what the other says. She is a widow in black; I wear lots of colors. I wonder what she thinks. She has a stern demeanor. I think about her as I return to the room and lie in bed.

Only later when I am leaving, I see she is charmed by my stories even if she does not know a word of English. Her soft side reveals itself; I am not just a stranger. I take nice pictures of her by the window in her small informal living room. She smiles, feels happy. This truly makes my day.

Her terrace invites; here I practice yoga and *pranayamas*. A cool shower sates, and then I am ready for the day. I sit in the room writing notes when I hear sounds. Milos has arrived; it is about 10:30 a.m. While he talks with Dora, I complete my notes and gather my things. I have chosen to wear a sarong and white t-shirt, hoping to be comfortable in the glaring heat. I think of staring into the eyes of lions and being consumed by their expanding glare.

I join them for a chat. She has been cutting beans; I had thought of helping her, but was involved with my morning *sadhana*. By the time I am ready, she is well-nigh done. Milos seems nervous as he speaks with Dora.

Soon, he is going to tell me that he wants to return to Athens because he must work on a project for the institution where he works. I will wonder how to change things around, but it is not going to work. I will suggest and detach myself, thinking of all this exertion of travel in scorching heat for just one day, and a few historical places to see. Then I will gladly let it go. No picnic at the great rock. No swimming. No holiday. *Ohi.*

"We'll go back," I will say with a finality that will impress me. There will not be any point in staying if one person isn't having a good time. It's too late for the gathering in Rafina (home of an Angeleno friend) and a logistical impossibility. I will be respectful of what must unfold.

Change in Plans

We visit his great-aunt, who gives us a ride to the village of Tinos. At that time the decision is to stay in Tinos until sundown, then swim and return by night. But by the time we reach Tinos, he changes his mind. I read Kazantzakis in the car, so entranced am I by the beauty of his writing, the power of his incisive connecting of time, tide, human triumphs and foibles, and his own presence in his enormous universe, so rich and magnificent. He makes the landscape come alive while I am in it. This book has traveled with me from Crete.

Here, the situation is a bit involved—so I surrender. Milos tries to prompt me to not read; "It's bad for your eyes to read in the car." I nod, smiling, but the book is too good to put down, a rich translation I am enjoying very much. Just a page more.

After Zena drops us off, he says again that he wants to return to Athens. It was already decided. Compliance sometimes is the better choice. If one person is in a spot, it's better to find a place of safety for both. So I say, "We'll go back...!"

He buys the return tickets, and we walk around town for a bit. We stop at a *taverna* and order *kalamari*, which turns out to be a bad choice, not as superior as at other places. We take a cab back to bring our things. I don't see the relatives again, but I spend some time with Dora, with whom I have stayed.

She is surprised and sorry that we are leaving so soon. She makes me coffee and sits with me. We converse without understanding each other. I see her eyes have opened to dancing at me with affection. Mine too. There are always nuggets in moments if we but choose to be present and care to connect.

Stella in Black...

The 73-year-old woman sits by the window looking at the over-hanging plants, the chink of blue sky hovering in between openings in the foliage. The heat settles in waves here and there. Insistent, it won't let go. The window reflects her face and the plants—it seems they are part of the one design. Then she turns her face ever so slightly and a small smile appears. It is shy, like a young girl looking at her lover, or remembering him.

She must be remembering something, because her eyes mist over even as they sparkle with a kind of playfulness. She is dressed completely in black. Outside is a group of Dutch and English tourists. Dressed casually, some are ready for a dip in the sea. Tressa prances in wearing a bikini and sarong clasped loosely around her waist. Her goggles round her neck, her hair coiled in a loose knot held together with a ribbon.

"Hey John," she says in a sing-song way, "let's...." John pulls his chair out and pats his knees. Tressa walks over to him and sits casually on his knees, while the others finish their late breakfast, coffee and all. John runs his fingers along her back. She is ticklish and squirms on his lap. Duffy makes a comment; others laugh. He looks around him and catches the image of Stella staring out the window. Duffy cranes his neck and

226

meeting eyes with Stella, he winks at her. Quite an odd group just arrived from the States on a soul-searching visit.

Stella pulls back. She cannot hear it all; the language is foreign to her, but she knows what is happening. She purses her lips and turns away. Reaching for the old chest, she opens it. Some letters fall out of the neat arrangement. She bends down to pick it up when her huge dog playfully trots over, but feeling her neglect, he plops down. The heat is too much for him.

She picks up the envelope and takes out the letter. Old dry petals fall out of the folded paper. Her hands tremble, she is nervous. A soft breeze blows momentarily and that is enough to make Stella take a quick deep breath in. At that very moment, Duffy appears at the open door. He stands looking at Stella, whose neatly tied hair has loosened and strands fall all over her face.

Stella does not realize Duffy is elegantly lining the doorway. She reads the letter from her dead husband. It is written in a graceful hand. These are notes of his desire for her as he sits in some bunker in the war. Stella feels all the old sexual feelings. Her eyes close as she remembers.

Those nights, those long nights waiting for Theo to return. His return. Each time he'd return from war, she'd be pregnant. She had five children by him. Each time she saw him, her body would become full, it would quiver, and the cups would fill up in the kitchen with magical water.

Stella's hands close tightly over the letter crumpling it as though it were the sheets under her as she consummated her desires and made her husband

227

happy. Her eyes are shut tightly; she does not hear the stirring near the door.

Duffy, the eternal photographer, wishes he had his camera with him—damn, where was his Nikon? Why did he leave it in his room? The room he rented from this woman. Never had he seen such passion, not even at the height of his love for Susan, from whom he was divorced for some seven years now. But he is intruding and he knows that. But he cannot help himself. He is transfixed.

The slumbering dog lets out a soft rumbling growl, and Stella comes out of her trance. In a trice though Duffy moves away from sight. Stella looks around her, wondering what it was that took her away and what brought her back. She seems to be taking stock of her surroundings.

She looks at her hands and realizes she still holds the letter. She straightens it and sees that she has also crumpled the photo along with it. At that moment, Duffy knocks gently on the door. Stella looks up and trying to gain composure, she nods.

He enters. His eyes are intense. He is moved to say something, but is silent. At the same time, he feels he has already betrayed her. He wants to love her or his dream of her. But he is a guest, a paying guest. He knows it is impossible. He wants to dream.

She motions him to a vacant chair. He sits down. She asks him what he wants. Duffy replies, "Nothing. May I just look at you?"

But Stella speaks nary a word of English, so she is perplexed.

228

Duffy wants to know why all the women are always in black. "Why do you wear black all the time?" He knows her husband has been gone for many years now. Why the lifelong mourning? He catches her reflection in the window: An image of stateliness, simmering passion coming undone. Something sterile covers the picture. He knows he had traveled in the tunnel to her past and seen her as she once was. As she still is. He'd like to go there with her.

Something in her demeanor tells him her decision is to remain in her shroud, in her little empire, contained in black.

Stella tells him she had five children. Her gestures are meaningful and he knows a few words in Greek. Enough to piece together broken bits of meaningful and meaningless sounds. He points to the picture. She nods. Then tells him the man in the picture was her husband and she was sorting through things in her box. He nods to say he has understood, even if he hasn't quite.

She asks if he would like some coffee. Duffy shakes his head. He ventures, "I'd like you...." She does not understand. She shrugs her shoulders. Duffy tries again. Would she go and walk with him this evening? He acts out his words. Stella turns rigid for a moment, then a smile wanders in very quickly and leaves as quickly. She does not say a word. She merely looks at him, then at her dog.

The late noon sun turns brighter as sounds of the guests from the patio suddenly filter in louder than before.

She turns to look out the window. A hint of a smile touches her lips. And suddenly, she is again gone.

But as Duffy gets up to go, she turns to look at him—this rakish man, with sandy blonde hair and lines that will become wrinkles. She turns to look at him, ever so slightly. And a small smile holds her transfixed, a single hand rises as though to stop time as it slowly faces her heart and stops.

A lone mosquito comes out of hiding and moves in the hot air looking for another place to rest in before darkness brings its other secrets.

Shifts in Time

Milos arrives at close to 5; the cab driver is dead on time. I say "goodbye" to the lovely elegant solemnly smiling Dora and thank her for her generous kindness and everything, even her stories. We leave for Tinos. I do not speak, nor wish to, and am not able to: my voice leaves me when I am deeply sad or overwhelmed by some emotion. Two little tears roll down my cheeks as we drive away. In silence everything that happens to me is invisible to everyone else. I remember Greece is buried. Something in me becomes buried at this moment. Or maybe it is unburying.

The rock waits for me, I whisper. Then I tell myself to not be melodramatic. What's the point, really? I feel complete because I am. I have a bowl full of little rocks, colorful ones in my living room—each has a history, some I have forgotten.

Milos is a little concerned at my silence. "Say something," he persists. I am not surprised; others in the past have been as well, as I am also known to be shy or reserved. Yes, I admit when I am not listened to, I have a tendency to withdraw into silence. And yes, I am feeling fatigue of being far from home. In my silence, much happens. In my silence I am full and complete. I have acknowledged my sadness at leaving this mysterious place so quickly, so randomly. I have no desire to say anything. I have no desire to know anything. I had simply wished to visit that big rock on the hillside. I have said enough.

This silence is not voluntary, but the voice of a being deep inside me.

The rock remains in my memory; for some sweet reason, that is good enough for now. The rock is immovable; I wish my mind could move even rocks. According to local lore, this rock is known for making marriages happen. People have asked for its blessing and their desires have been fulfilled. Everywhere people seek such blessings and affirmations from trees, rocks, pools of water, and shrines. Our longing for such connections unites us. Yes, we claim to be so different and are continually at war. But we are more alike than not.

I will miss the embrace of this rock; my desires will be manifest in the most divine way. We drive by the tower built for the pigeons, a sentimental structure of the people of Tinos.

From Tara's Notebook

Soon, Tara will speak. She has a few words to say; they are endless. These new vibrations. The Oracle at Delphi has confirmed a new poetry for the golden age. The Oracle has sent word through invisible ones with wings to await Tara's gaining her voice. The gods are with those who guide, with those who make good lives. It is said. It is done. So it is...!

Kindling desire
floats from many points
of eternity to arms
of embrace opening
wide like wings
wonder trembles in my being

Eyes widen enfold the sun
your eyes whose longing
makes moist the sand
below our naked feet

Pray child, pray for innocence
to never leave your side
Pray... claim your singular wild heart

We leave our bags at the tourist shop and stroll through the village. We do not visit the Panagia, one of the most famous cathedrals to the Virgin Mary, but we wander around pretty shops. I have tasted a twinge of sadness at my limitations, but now I am mellow. I buy Milos a gift of myrrh and frankincense. He calls it *"limani."* He has never before burnt any. So many firsts are a world expansion for this neophyte in search of purpose but unwilling to reflect on it.

What of me? What in me is new that I have not known before? Will I realize it?

Sometimes, it is safer to stay within the confines of a known world, stay within our limitations, but it cannot be exciting to do so. Human passions would simmer and be pushed down away from view. A life would be half-lived. Wouldn't Jupiter have us travel far and wide? Saturn too? Far from home. So they tell me when they read my map of the skies, all computed mathematically. So they tell me. It is partly true.

We walk around the town then sit on some wall. A man and a woman are taking pictures. He wears a pair of women's sandals with high heels. It is comical. I take pictures of Milos against the backdrop of street vendors on this street noisy with the heat; this is the last of Tinos. I miss seeing the church for which this island is famous. I feel complete. Perhaps, another Mother Maria would be too much for me.

Silence savors me.

I am still not able to speak. But I want to get into line for the boat soon to depart. Milos wants to stay in a cool place, under the fan in the ticket shop. So we do. This means that we do not get good seats anywhere on the boat. It is a mad scramble. He carries both our bags. Remembering what coffee grain diviner Stavros had said about my bags, I gesticulate that we take them in with us. Coffee grounds guide my actions.

On the Boat Again

We find some horrid chairs in a restaurant that smells greasy, fried. Neither of us likes this place. I go up on the deck to look for places for us. Eventually, we go up on the deck. I don't know when, but somehow my voice begins to return. I am still reading Kazantzakis' *Report to Greco*. Maybe he brings my voice back. His need to insist on his experience; his passion for all the levels of his being to spill into words perhaps stirs my voice to emerge again. It is still soft.

Milos has made himself comfortable besides me. He is attentive once in a while. He checks on the bags from time to time. He points out certain suspicious characters he believes are gypsies who might swipe "anything from anyone at any time." He is observant; I like that. If he had been with me in the Metro at the Akropolis, I wouldn't have been the target of thieves.

This fine quality in him makes me feel safe. This realization fills me with a sense of joy. I'm not sure why. Everything seems unreal. I am to leave in a few days for Los Angeles. But it's nice to know this feeling. Safety is a good feeling; having felt it one can record and recall it when needed.

We sit on the deck. I read a bit now and then. We look at the sky. He wants to do a drawing with me. We sketch. It is interesting what is happening. I am following him in whatever he wants to do; this is a reversal of sorts. Earlier he had made himself available if I wanted to go anywhere. I decide to let go and do whatever it is he wishes. Giving up control and moving with another's flow brings a new perspective to one's experience of life. I feel richer and freer for it.

From time to time, he walks around the boat but always lets me know when he wishes to walk. When the boat stops at Sferia, a town known for its unique college campus, he points to the beauty of the edge of town, floating in the sea.

Now the sun will be in our faces, he says, so we should move. I think that the boat will turn in the other direction anyway. He insists. I have surrendered, so we go to the other side of the boat. We are in the sun when we leave the shores.

233

A young woman sits not far from me. Milos says she looks sad. I am a bit puzzled at his interest in her loneliness. Is it really his loneliness? I leave to walk and stretch. When I return, I find they have been chatting. I quietly return to my seat. She is a student on the island on her way home for the holidays. We wish one another good luck. She leaves. Milos returns. It is a lyrical and curious dance in the long arms of the sun skirting around the islands.

We enjoy the rushing waters, singular autonomous beings, each moved by a single reason to inspire happiness. Our journeys take us in many directions and sometimes bring us to friends who must be our mirrors. Once we've learned something about ourselves, the purpose has been fulfilled. We let go then, in respect and affection for our singular purpose and journey, for having learned lessons. Letting go is an artful process we must learn well. Some attachments create bonds we don't need in our lives. Sylvia Plath, the poet, had written, *"Dying is an art / I have done it so many times..."*

Traveling companions must be true to their destiny. Perhaps, we will communicate again, perhaps not. Sometimes, there is no reason to. I will leave in two days. I recall my resistance about visiting Tinos, but I had come. Much had happened, much hadn't. It's respectful to acknowledge our circles of influence—how we each affect one another, so we can sculpt our lives with the ambiguity of honesty and tenderness.

I am reminded again that what we often like in another are qualities similar to ours, and what we don't know are the voices and faces in the shadows. There are great differences between us; I am an active person interested in various pursuits; he has a laziness that keeps him cocooned in a small world. I have opened his windows a few times—he has exclaimed at the newness of things. I am moving with the flow. The sound of the boat churning in the water takes over; people chatter.

Am I liberating myself from myself? Or am I merely uncovering in order to re-cover? Words. How easily they can confound us! We must be in integration with our inner hearts, through words and away from them. Silence is a good friend.

234

The sun is setting—I take pictures. Orange machinery in the foreground lends an interesting flavor. It's not bright enough to read, so Kazantzakis has to be bagged.

Feeling pangs of hunger, we go inside to Goody's Café where he buys fries and a hamburger. I get hot water in my traveling mug and use a bag of tea. Always feels good to drink hot tea. Although a snack would have been welcome, nothing tantalizes me in the hot crowded space. Several people sit looking at the boat that vigorously ploughs the black sea; we find some chairs and sit. I sing a song in Hindi. He likes it and asks if it is a love song. I say everything is about love. I tell him the singer says let me live in the shadows of your eyelashes. Everything is about love.

We are back at the deck covered by a black sky. The boat moves on scudding in darker waters. Tiring of this aimless walking, we sit. I sense Milos' nervous energy. Suddenly, he gets up and comes to my other side and lifts me in his arms as a buccaneer would. Now what is this? He puts me down gently to sit where I was sitting. That is all. What was that about? I ask him. He says nothing. I don't remember ever being lifted like this. What is going on in him I do not know and decide not to. I had my Reagan with Maggie in his arms moment! Better still Clark Gable with Vivien Leigh! He is a small guy and I am bigger—this incongruity is hilarious and tender. I feel shaken; the moment has passed.

In the distance are approaching lights. We look out over the dark stretch. I wonder how many stories are layered in the waters; how many people have traveled here back and forth for how many centuries. Water is the element of creating, of dying, cleansing and of forgetting.

The boat meets the dock. We gather our luggage. In the crowd, we are among the last to disembark. It takes us some time to get a taxi. But we get one and are on our way home. He shows me his art and tells me a little about his project. I understand that he had wanted to feel safe about sharing his work. And more importantly, he had wanted to complete his project. He drives me home; I wish him good journeys and the reaching of his destinations. I thank him for his kindness. We say "good night" to one another.

I am at the door of the house waiting for someone to open it. It is late and folks might have retired. But doors are to be opened. I enter—it's nice to feel the ground slowly becoming solid again. They ask about my visit. I long for home. Warm fragrant tea calms my insides before I go to sleep. Sunday is another day. I feel resolute to not let anything get me down, for I am in this in-between place. I sleep well but wake early.

The strangeness of the day crawls on my skin. I feel like doing nothing. So I rest, eat, call Stavros in Athens and Nicolaus in California. Meropi will come in the middle of the day. Thaleia, the eternal mother, makes *kalamari* and rice for me. Stavros is ready to come, but I'm not ready to see him. I spend the day cleaning up, reflecting, and packing my stuff. Everything must be ready for my travel tomorrow to avoid last minute stress. Meropi and I eat; the rice is good but not as good as the last time Thaleia made it. White rice tastes better than brown rice, which needs to cook longer, but Thaleia disagrees with me and is a bit offended. Then smiles.

Images of my days here crowd and jostle one with the other: I wonder what more of me have come undone in my own re-cognition. Caught in a conundrum, I feel a bit stuck. How can the mind and heart of me be content if I am wanting for its opposite when I might learn to enjoy what is occurring in the present? I smile at the thought of having, not having, and the possibility of having something or being something or someone else. Yes to be okay with the existence of all these at one time would be far better than fighting with myself. Then I think of existence, non-existence, and the possibility of integrating the All-ness of all moments of experience in the one moment and bring myself to greater enjoyment of myself.

I know when I tell my friend Nikolaus about my time in his home country, about making choices, about experiences with different people, he will say cheerfully, "Well you can't do all the beautiful things all at once." Right, Nikolaus. Everything that we do is beautiful in the moment. Then we have the memory of it. Truly, when I tell him about the Cyclops and the Mad Hatter, Nikolaus will say, "You've had a peculiar time in Greece." I will assure him all was grand. Of course, and beautiful, *Irie, Changa...!*

Clanking of dishes in the kitchen brings me to the present. I realize that what has been most peculiar is dealing with Mad Melpo (Paris, one of the boys, calls her that). In the afternoon, I go up to her room to see how she is doing and am horrified at how utterly filthy it is. She's had a crisis all day. She has been trying to dry up the water that she poured on her equally dirty dog in the bedroom. She is a crisis.

Why Athanas insists on keeping the poor mangy dog is also absurd, especially since no one takes care of it, and Mad Melpo's room is unsafe. She can slip, fall, break her fragile bones; then what would they do? There seem to be gaps in communication or understanding. Am I sounding like I am reaching tenderly for a short fuse?

When love is all that matters,
why are we lax in its remembering?

It's not that a flower forgets
Or the sea does not rage.

It's simply that we take too long
to make it right...isn't it?

> *When people start to disappear*
> *see light fading into twilight.*

> *memory cannot replace*
> *flesh blood smell smile;*

> *only sadness sews itself*
> *again in our bones skin hair*

> *how our fingertips caress*
> *beloved voice...*

237

"Death does not concern us, because as long as we exist, death is not here. And when it does come, we no longer exist. "

~ Epicurus

Chapter 11 ~ Resolutions Between Worlds

The story of generations is the same the world over: mothers of sons have a hold on their boys; Thaleia has seen the unpleasantness of a possessive mother-in-law and a husband who has pandered to his mother. So Thaleia leaves Mama Melpo to her depressants and does not visit her upstairs. The son-husband is not home.

Feeling partly familial and thinking of my great-grandmother, I take Mama Melpo, the beautiful woman suffering a form of dementia, for a walk in the afternoon. I experience more glimpses into a mind so far away from present reality. I learn as I direct this lady around that I have to be firm with boundaries, both mine and hers, for she can wander into her mind's wilderness and indulge in dramas. Bringing her back would be beyond me. I could incur her wrath, a stream of invective, wild accusations. What would the neighbors think who have seen her for so much longer?

I guide her back and, once inside, try to placate Mama Melpo with some juice mixed with powdered pills; this she drinks gratefully, but it seems to have no effect on her. She is much too feisty and driven. It is only later that she gives in and goes to her room but for a little while only. Thaleia asks me to take her a plate of food, which I do. Melpo is thankful but won't eat any; she throws the food on the floor for the dog, who refuses to eat any of this.

The still wet floor is littered with a variety of foods, paper-wrappings of many vintages, dirt. The poor dog lives in this mess. A woman is losing her ground and her land. Her land is losing her.

239

Nino walks into the kafé with a wide grin sticking to her like a crinkled frill on the edge of a dancing dress. Eyes are wide, almost guileless. She looks around and finds a small table. She sees Carla, a young woman from overseas. Nino only knows that Carla is not from here. "Do you like Greece?" she asks Carla who sits drinking coffee at the table with a checkered cloth. Carla nods. Nino nods happily. She repeats her question. Carla repeats her answer. Nino looks around, brushes crumbs off the table and looks up at Carla, smiles. She repeats her question. Carla nods her answer and drinks her coffee. She looks at the clock; she's waiting for Dimitris to pick her up and take her to the station.

Nino beckons the waiter. Spiros rrives. "Ena kafé," she says and then, pointing to Carla, "Does she like Greece?" Spiros is a jolly fellow and he nods giving her a big grin. Nino is placated as she sits down and looks round her with a faintly mutinous air as though she owns the place and no one may defy her on any account. She drinks her coffee and pours the remains on the saucer and leaves it for some time. She looks over at Carla and grins at her. Carla is curious and walks over to sit with Nino.

Nino smiles at her happily. "You like it here?" Carla nods. Nino continues, "Ne, it is nice here." Nino takes Carla's cup and swirls it round and turns it over on her saucer. She then picks it up and reads.

"You have long journey in front of you ... you like Greece? It's good ... you will work hard and then you will let it go. Very soon. You will go and you will come back. Just like that ... you go, you come. Hmm ... you will be always protected ... Husband? Where's he?"

Carla shrugs her shoulders and shakes her head. "I also don't know where mine is... he got up one day... never came back...." Nino tells Carla. Spiros shakes his head in passing and reminds Nino that her husband was dead. And that she had led the funeral procession. Carla is somewhat confused. Spiros returns with a tray of coffees and whispers, "She forgets everything... sometimes even how to go home ... she lives two seconds from here." He points out the door. There.

Carla looks at Nino who taps the table and rocks at the same time as though in a trance. "Nino ... Nino?" ventures Carla. Nino comes out of her reverie and gives Carla the strangest look that frightens her. "Who are you? Go home ... go home you ...what are you doing here? This is my land. My dead live here...." Nino spits out at Carla who is taken aback and gets up. Nino clears the table with a swoop of her hand; the coffee cups fall to the floor.

Spiros comes to the rescue only to be at the receiving end of Nino's ranting. He tries to placate her; Carla steps away. Spiros picks up the broken china and walks Carla to the other end of the room. "She's a little crazy ... don't worry. Is not personal. She has forgotten everything.... They say she did something terrible in her village ... too bad for me to say ... maybe she did ... or no... I don't know.... But... who knows...?" He shrugs his shoulders to his ears and drops his hands eyebrows raised.

"Forgotten everything? What do you mean? Her family...?!" Carla wonders.

"They are there...now...don't worry...I go send her back," so saying Spiros goes to his phone and calls Nino's family. In the meanwhile, Nino looks at everyone in the taverna with a sweet smile as though the demons

241

in the psyche had left her in peace. She is not the same person from two minutes ago.

Carla steals a glance at Nino and looks away but Nino does not miss it. She walks over to Carla and runs her hand over the young woman's head and nods with admiration. "My child, you look just like my little girl...how you have grown up." Carla smiles but is hesitant. She steals a glance at Spiros who hums back and forth as he delivers the sandwiches and also keeps watch. He is used to Nino's outbursts. In fact, so are his customers—the regular ones. Carla catches a conversation from the neighboring table.

"Poor thing...what must she keep in her...that screams like this to be let out...?" asks the woman.

"Who knows...old age is a little like old land...ancient places have secrets no one can ever find out Speaking of being buried, did you go to Petro's funeral?" says the man. "Petro's funeral? What are you saying? Petro? Our Petro?" the woman is aghast.

"You didn't know...?" the man is stunned.

"I've been away in the village for long...are you sure our Petro Lamakis...?" The man nods as the woman sits back, suddenly pale. Her eyes mist over as her hand goes limp on her lap.

Carla looks up at Nino who sits down and takes Carla's hand in her own. "You like it here? Yes?" asks Nino as she looks into Carla's eyes. "Stay here then...bring it back to life...I'm dying," Carla takes a deep breath. Spiros comes over and says, "Now don't trouble our guests, Mama..." "I am not trouble...I am asking her to stay and bring us back from the dead. All of us...all who are dead can return. No?" and she looks around.

242

Seeing no one paying her any attention, she starts to whine and intones, "Oh this heat...what am I going to do? It's so hot. Spiros, bring me some ice parakalo...Cool her down or what will she think?"

"Ah...old age and summer heat..." Spiros muses as he goes to welcome new customers. In the meantime, Carla sits under the constant caresses of the old crone whose mind wanders between crevices of memory that resist salvation, that want to be forgotten somewhere in air, remain irretrievable.

Perhaps this is what happens when there's too much to remember. You forget it all. If you're smart enough. And Carla remembers her own grandmother in her home country, sitting on an old bed made of rope. The old lady with eyes that shone like coal through film of cataract, her admonishments, her reprimands, her orders. And Carla wonders if old people stand not for themselves, but as agents of their land, its traditions, its history, its language—everything that it could have become and didn't.

She reaches out and runs her fingertips on Nino's face. On her wrinkles. Nino smiles. "This is my country," she says. "You like it?" Carla nods. "When I die, I want be buried in my church. You will tell them that...don't forget." "No, I will tell them...I won't forget," Carla promises the old woman.

"...The summer heat has won its way and nothing wants to remember but nothing lets you forget..." Carla recites.

Nino does not understand what Carla says, but she nods in agreement. She is part of the conspiracy that she created. It's all in her mind.

When Lands Age

The elderly in our communities stand for more than themselves. They are agents of the land. The lines on their faces are not just age wrinkles; these are parchment lines of the whole history of the land. If they forget something, does it suggest that the land on which they have walked has lost something from its consciousness? Or that it is buried and wants to forget something? Perhaps, the land needs to forget its excesses, its indulgences, and guilt over bad behaviors, perhaps the anger and pain of relationships. After all land is memory.

Perhaps the elders suffer guilt of what they have done to their progeny—or not done for themselves. Ancestors keep playing their terrible dramas through us. And it falls on our shoulders to set matters right, so we can rebuild what was handed to us: broken walls, windows, wings.

Having seen much of this, I am familiar with the possessive mother-spoilt son dynamic. It hurts men and their ability to be intimate; they recreate their mothers in the women they marry and destroy their women's self-worth! Such dynamic makes the men poor martyrs and grand manipulators. My sympathies are with Thaleia. But why am I in the middle of this? Because I have seen this in my family and wondered why people marry. What I wish for is marriage as communion, as resonance, as coherence: Love.

A marriage is communication, love, surrender to each other's greatness and gifts, sorrows and vulnerabilities. True partnership is show of support so each is fulfilled, whole even in vulnerable moments, especially then. Forever. For then we each is the beloved—this is my vision. Nothing less. The Rock at Tinos has heard this.

The banging on doors continues upstairs...Mad Melpo can't let go. The only way Thaleia can deal with this is to visit friends.

She leaves somewhat in a huff, needing respite from all this drama. The world has been on her shoulders too long.

Let us liberate our elders from our limitations. Let us simply practice a purpose to be happy. Somehow.

Feeling caught between this world and my desire to return to my life in Los Angeles, I reflect in silence. I socialize very little but realize that moments with a few people who enjoy giving and listening are fulfilling and satisfying, like my time with Meropi, Milos, even Stavros. Will I miss them? For a few moments. Perhaps. Then I will be subsumed with life's passions, writing about my many-splendored moments, wondering about human purpose and destiny, making miracles, feeling sorrow, building new things, dreaming, and learning the delighting art of surrender. It is such a dance.

This Sunday, however, I give in to the unfolding of events, a state in the family dynamic. I bribe Mama Melpo so I can also have some peace. She is happy when I bring her drinks and cold water; in return, she stays quiet for a while. In the meantime, Thaleia returns from her visit visibly happier, and we share some rice with vegetables.

Soon Meropi arrives; she is keen to take me to the town for a drink with her friends. Despite my sense of unease, I agree to go with her and her friend, George, also from Albania. We will meet at Dafni station. Meropi goes to her place to get changed.

I had forgotten to call Stavros to say we couldn't get together today. When I call, he has made other plans. It is my fault and I know it, but life had other plans. So I am on this very strange ride, one I will regret. The airlessness of the Neos Cosmos Metro greets me. When the train rolls in, I am standing at the exact spot where the door opens and Meropi stands in the train. This is uncanny. I enter. We are on our way.

The moment I see George standing by a shop, I know this is a mistake. His lackadaisical appearance and manner, his strange elongated face with a square prognathous jaw, trigger a strange repulsion to a Dickensian world of excess. Almost immediately, he launches into a diatribe extolling his virtues. I am stunned at this aggrandized revelation of arrogance. He is an energy vampire, and I will soon request to conclude the evening, as I am ready to travel early the next day. We drive in his car, but the restaurant by the sea he takes us to is closed for business.

I find a public phone and call a friend in California. I need his familiar voice. He is so happy to hear me that he almost falls off his chair laughing.

We leave for another restaurant nearby. I sing to please myself. We go to this loud smoky place that makes my throat sore. This begins to irritate me, and I feel violated, my boundaries threatened. He is so concerned about telling us how much fun he has that I wonder at his empty life, lacking substance and bliss. I order coffee, he alcohol. Meropi appears cowed down. It makes me wonder what power he has over her. Suddenly, I miss Stavros—we would have had a charming reflective evening, speaking of mythos and ethos instead of living a strangely disquieting version of its raucous emptiness. As George continues to indulge in his excesses, I find I am unable to breathe. To avoid the boring details, I fast forward, and finally, we leave; by now, Meropi is uncomfortable. I wonder what her intentions had been.

The road to the Metro station is long, very long. I pray that this one be short. I am not going to meet a Lestrygonian or a Cyclops; I am with one and it is taking too long to be free of him. When we finally reach Dafni and I get out of the car, I find I can suddenly breathe again—this is instantaneous. This is magic. What a release from the strangest albatross I'd worn round my neck. I cannot wait to walk away. We bid farewell. We depart. I tell Meropi a little bit about my experience; I know she feels badly. I assure her all will be well. She starts to wonder about him. He has been, thus far, just someone with whom she could go to a bar.

I settle in for the night, but busy demons keep me awake, sleepless with an overactive mind.

Unraveling Resolutions

It's very early. I drink my warm sweet tea and wash up, then walk to the market to make calls. When I return, Thaleia is getting ready for work. We chat for a few minutes.

She wants me to get my new long dress fixed so I can wear it. She wants me to take it to her seamstress down the street. This woman who watches out for the whole family, deals with tensions of being a homemaker and an office worker, waves at me and leaves. This is the last time I will see her leave for work, I think with a tiny twist in my heart.

I turn around and return to the kitchen with Mama Melpo, who chatters away in Greek. I make breakfast. The doorbell rings; Milos comes to pick up some papers. He asks if I am free in the evening for coffee. I say we could have coffee after my meetings, and I must sleep early tonight for I leave at 4:30 a.m. He nods and leaves.

As usual I eat some *yaourti*, a last fine taste; but I can't finish it.

Meropi is not in a good mood. She takes me to the seamstress, who cannot fix my dress in one day—a lime green dress reminiscent of cool summer evenings. Thaleia calls and asks her to take me to another woman who does the work. The seamstress takes in the dress and makes it fit on me very well. I beam like a cool summer day.

Back in the house, I speak with Stavros who will visit me in the evening. We set a time. As it so happens, he comes later, after I've left with Milos to go to the Plaka. He brings a small gift and plans on meeting us later.

We reach the Plaka but the shop, Ermione, is closing. I am unable to buy a very lovely lyrical mermaid sculpture that I'd liked. The red dress has also gone; the woman is closing shop when we arrive. When departure is nigh, doors start to close.

Walking along, we arrive at Costas' Antique Shop. I buy a few small Cycladic sculptures. I don't listen to Milos when he tells me to buy only real copies of the authentic Cycladic pieces, like the one of a man playing a harp. I think I won't regret it later. Some pieces resemble the style, but may not be copies of originals—this is what Milos says. One is of a woman stretching up and reaching backwards to the ground. I like the simplicity of this piece, but I miss the man with the harp. He plays in my mind's eye. I decide to listen more carefully to words of people who know.

I buy more of those eyes of blue, black and white glass used to ward off evil. Make nice little gifts.

On a whim, I suggest we go to the terrace *kafé* of Hotel Plaka. I want to see it again—it is where I spent some evenings with the group of Prometheusa screenwriters, with Seamus, Brady, Anita and others. It is where we had our last meeting and gave our presentations about a month ago in June. Today is the 22nd of July, this is my last evening here. I wish to revisit an old familiar place and also say "goodbye" to Caroline, the English woman who runs a bar on the terrace at this hotel.

My last view of the Akropolis! I stand enthralled, breathing in the beauty of this grand creation, built with fine attention to lines and meeting points. I wonder if there was any astrological consideration in its planning. There might have been. It glows goldenly in the night sky, a cover hugging the city. The sky is a conglomerate of nightlights like glowing eyes: stars over Tinos.

We buy a frappe and a cup of tea into which I pour Angostura bitters. We sit on reclining chairs and make small talk. There isn't much to say. Our worlds and experiences are distant and different. Our mythical worlds do not mesh; there is a different story for each generation. But it is nice to unwind here high up on the terrace.

The music from a nearby *taverna* floats up here, the tourists down below at the various inns, the winking lights, people on the terrace make a fine weave. I close my eyes and everything seems to become one sound.

I smile inside and think time cannot and will not end; it is the bottomless cup of brimming. Life is wonderful when we meet and recognize our center. Nothing else matters, but the moment, which is always complete, in spite of distractions in our minds, fragments in our psyche, wanderings in our imagination. Everything happens concurrently in synthesis.

I open my eyes and Milos asks why people go away. I say because we are butterflies. We laugh silently. I never made it to the island of Paros, where I had dreamed of writing a story filled with the glow, the flirtatious dance of butterflies.

We are silent. I see how fascinating it is when people can speak frankly about nothing at all and that stars glitter in night sky. That's what matters.

Story of the Sea as it's Meant to Be...

Tara's fingers trace the pictures of the setting sun—it's a brilliant orange, a burnt orange, a shade that always twists her up. It shimmers in the darkening blue waters, which will soon swallow it up. She has no tears for the sea. She whispers, "the temple of the rock waits for me...I know. I surrender...I say goodbye."

Tara's heart is full—Nikos' eyes are full of moonlight sprinkling its blessings over the land. Besides a gigantic bush near the sea. Very near the sea. And Nikos' voice asking, "Ti...? Taroula...ti? Tara turns her head when he says, "open your eyes." "They are open," she says. Very open, looking at him. His smile drops its sweetness into her eyes.

Nearby the sea delivers. "Why do people always go away?" he asks. Nearby the sea takes away. This is the story of the sea when the moon is full. When their eyes are full, language falls apart—becomes unnecessary. It's just the heart's longing wrapped in moonlight that hearts can swallow, so they may remember how the sea sings in the dark. Tara must leave at the crack of dawn when coffee filters through to warm a heart emptying its contents onto paper.

Then we who remain grope among rocks for stories about stars that must have fallen, dancing to the song of the sea.

Tara and Niko do not leave footprints in the sand; All That Is is surely swallowed by the sea. As it was and as it is always truly meant to be.

249

Conclusions Without Endings

Each person is a rich magnificent story. A single glance is an eternity of story.

I have said my farewell to everyone in the family, my generous hosts. I have said goodbye to Stavros. I have said farewell to Meropi and Tzimis. I have said goodbye to Mama Melpo; I wonder how she will get by. I have lain to rest that part of me that was ready to be "lost" and resolved. Farewell, dear heart.

I am ready for my return trip to New York, final destination Los Angeles. What do I long for now? What are my new dreams? I wonder what in me will emerge. I try to cover up a familiar emptiness in me, but it is too late. It has already been uncovered. There is no turning back.

Athens suddenly feels like magic.

My last ride to the airport kindly offered by Naos, an associate of Thaleia and father of Eudora, who is friend of Paris, Bion, and Damali, seems like a ride on the back of the winged horse—it is smooth as the gold and silver that slips in unawares pushing away the night—I think of ancient stories all over the world.

They are about comings and goings, relentless unceasing movement, our transience from birth to another birth.

They are about longings that make us wonder about belonging.

What of the universal heart? Ancient poetry, all our mythologies will surely reconstruct this universal heart. Not its specific words, but its interwoven strata of being filtering into layers of becoming from some unidentified world into this one. Pure consciousness, I discover, is ordinary state.

Love is the glue that holds universes together. This is magic. I lean back in my seat on the plane and close my eyes.

Suddenly, the plane has become Pegasus, the great white winged horse, flying smoothly over land and sea. Taking me home, wherever home is. There is no rest or stasis; we keep moving in order to find home—movement inward and outward is the story of journeys.

I have returned from Greece—I haven't. I didn't write the screenplay I had intended to, for I didn't stay on an island long enough to do so; I was the island in search of my ley lines and my centers.

Down below, I see Los Angeles arriving, a city that seems to lack spontaneous closeness, a city demarcated by the murky transience of emotional lines and longings, a city also by a body of water, one rougher than that around Athens. But she is also a city of seekers, artists, creators, energy workers, spiritualists dodging dogma, idealists, people wanting to make a difference, self-righteous ones and corrupt ones, dreamers and more meeting in a depot of diverse cultures and points of view, sometimes ghettoized sometimes merging...like any metropolis urged to self-discovery.

The city of angels offers her brand of wisdom and disparateness, kindness and violence, for distances are vast both physical and emotional. She invites for her sweet ocean breezes, splintering beaches, mountains close by, for her bar and café culture, temples, places of spirit to worship, places of body worship where dwell gatherers of artifacts in a culture of isolation.

Everything is a brand. Mall culture with mass-produced everything is a veritable stupefier, which has made people become selfie-obsessed while they romance items from cultures all over the world. In order to discover commonality, why do we erase cultural uniqueness? This samification (sic) of things is not commonality.

Today we re-create ourselves with mass-produced digitized images or icons of antiquity, which may be now made of plaster or China-made plastic.

...to make things work out well and to do good, do we have to disappear?

251

Post Script ~ 1

Dear Reader: Cultural re-creations never end. The unfolding of selves never ends. How shall we learn to care when our nostalgia is ultimately for a self, which may or may not have ever existed? Does nostalgia evoke the archetypal and ancient self in the arriving future? Is every second a secret life revealing itself in parts? Do we rush in search of that which is always here though hidden?

I wanted to lose myself and gained more than I imagined. I am learning to deal with what is old and new in me. This, too, is one of the secrets in the lives of butterflies. The story I had come to write has written me, but not itself. This will have to wait: *The Secret Story of Butterflies.*

lingering in our hearts' many chambers
we long fragmented and whole
shall we discover what truly
nourishes our soul...?

What do butterfly wings teach us
that far is near
nearer than we imagine—?
    if not this, what else?
And near is very far very far away

Greece is magnificent, as are all ancient lands, reminding us of our eternity, our multi-layered selves. Let us not lose ourselves—it's so easy to do. Circe, Nausicaa, the Cyclops, and others are all here, as are spirits and intoxicants.

Illusions and manipulations can confound and steal us from ourselves. Let us take special care to not forget, for the starkly woven materialism of any culture can confound. Let us dance in continual becoming. Then what we are nostalgic for—the archetypal parts of us that Greece evokes—may reawaken in us our richness.

During my travels, I witnessed Greece falling to economic woes, in debt to the world for what it had lost. Heinous acts of bankers and politicians result in much waste. Actions of control and destruction continue. How much more practical and cheap it would be to allow for wisdom to have its say in the weave of new structures and relationships.

Is not purpose of human destiny to realize its greatest potential—to allow each one to emerge in fullness, capacity to love fiercely, handsomely, and wholesomely?

Even if it means now to acknowledge the end of things that cannot heal, but have done their part, and welcome that which is newly self-arising to be nourished by Areté, Eirene, Eros, Agape, and Sophia.

from...The Book of Wisdom

This verse is by one devoted to Sophia; perhaps, it is you!

10.
ὑπὲρ ὑγίειαν καὶ εὐμορφίαν ἠγάπησα αὐτήν, καὶ
προειλόμην αὐτὴν ἀντὶ φωτὸς ἔχειν, ὅτι ἀκοίμητον τὸ ἐκ
ταύτης φέγγος.

I loved Her more than beauty and good health,
and I chose to have Her rather than light,
because Her radiance never ceases.

Post Script ~ 2

Sublimations

1.
Is our evolution a movement
from one technology to another?
Do we recreate the same forms
in narratives we think are new?

2.
Flirtation with immortality reveals
gods dying to be reborn – rising
and falling swells of civilization.

It's all the same, my great-grandmother
used to say, nodding wisely, her head covered
with a white shawl, mole peering on her nose.
She would always smile, even when serious.

Encircled by Time, we share skies, stories.
We stub our toes, take pictures,
wonder at wisdom of stillness
like that of rocks, pristine story tellers.

When wind kisses rock, there are songs
fire crackling, water flowing, steam rising.

3.
Do we dance fearlessly to a different name?
Does a new name free us?

Is knowing oneself an unknowing?

Is liberation rapture? Look me in the eyes.
I walk in and out of doors meeting my buried
selves like parts of Greece crumbling.

4.
Suffering is noble, some say. It strengthens us.
But Greece, I say, is buried. Like we all are.

Do we ignite cords of joyful wisdom
when we reveal our innermost self?

Is realizing our inner-power creative
as is dissolution for the precious to arise?

Liquid fire kissing air becomes earth and song.
May we be guardians of all this!

Ancients wished we'd savor moments
that arise in us as love, sweetness of fresh breath.

Breathe life into every hand, live in simplicity,
give up suffering; let it transmute into joy.

5.
Joy can never be in excess. She stirs
        Soul's golden mean
Buddha's middling ways, Christ's simplicity
Hindu's way of bliss, faith of the Muslim,
mid-line of Sufi whirling as does Gaia.

May our self be subsumed in Beauty. Truth.
Harmony – Apollonian blues, sonata, *raaga*.
        Tender pleasures.
Scintillating – subversive – supernal.

Muses! Become us as we become you
continually in this dance of recovery.

Come to me I implore – I see with your eyes,

I wear your wheels in my ear lobes.
You, me, and Time roll into
and out of civilizations' rapacious ways

Let us follow Artemis, the Vedic Aranyani
through forests we must now embrace.

6.
Wait! Before then, I confess I have burned
in summer's fiery pot, cooled in blue roving waters

of many world seas, breathed life
of winds over lands fertile – now drying.

In the in-between spaces, I have held hands
with words, whose sounds have taken me
to a foraging of *Ur* tongues. Oh, I love trees.

They have blessed me before we were ever born –
you and I. I hear them in your heart and mine.

Something new is stirring. Listen.
How delicate are drops of fresh rain.

Can anything be the same ever again?

7.
My India stirs forever in me syllables
like a coiled serpent – sleepless – blinking!

Parashakti—May all our lands awaken in longing:
flutes, cellos, black soil, rugged prayers, drums.

So many antiquities in my bones
call wild-tenderly to remember them!

I wished Greece to free me.
I'm not sure what she has done.

About the Author

Ambika Talwar

Creative Vision for Changing Times
Author * Healer * Artist * Teacher * *Ecstatic Poet*

AMBIKA TALWAR is an India-born author, wellness consultant, artist, and educator whose vision is to realize her sacred destiny and invite others to find their brilliance. Insights gleaned through life challenges have prompted her to make her poetry a call to action. Composed in the ecstatic tradition, her poetry is a "bridge to other worlds." She has authored *Creative Resonance: Poetry—Elegant Play, Elegant Change* and also *4 Stars & 25 Roses (poems for her father)*. She is published in *Kyoto Journal, Inkwater Ink - vol. 3; Chopin with Cherries; On Divine Names; VIA-Vision in Action*; in *Poets on Site* collections; *St. Julian Press; Tower Journal, Tebot Bach, Life & Legends*, and others; has interviewed with KPFK; has recorded poems for the Pacific Asia Museum in Pasadena, California.

She won the Best Original Story award for her film *Androgyne* in Huy, Belgium; she wrote, produced and directed it. She asserts it is time for creative visionaries to offer narratives that change our worldview, and the big film studios must play a part in this transformation.

As an intuitive-spiritual healer, she practices *IE*:Intuition-Energetics™, a fusion of modalities, sacred geometry, and creativity principles. This full spectrum healing clears diverse obstructions, illnesses, and brings clients to ease and wholeness. *"Both poetry and holistic practices work beautifully together, for language is intricately coded in us through all time and dimensions,"* she notes.

An English professor at Cypress College, Ca, she lives in Los Angeles, Ca and New Delhi, India.

For book readings, healing workshops, and individual or group healing consultations, please contact her at: luminousfields@gmail.com

Web site: http://creativeinfinities.com
Download *My Prayer for You*. Listen to it any time.

Other Books, Essays, and Poems
By Ambika Talwar

"Singing Flutes & Poetics of Longing" An essay in *Poetry as a Spiritual Practice: Illuminating the Awakened Woman.* (2016) Edited by Catherine Ghosh and others. Golden Dragonfly Press.

"Vision of Surrender" A poem in *Identity & Anonymity: An Artful Anthology* (2016) with Susannah Campbell, Judy Chicago, Vincent Tavani, Loren Talbot and others. Edited by Jonathan Talbot, Leslie Fandrich and Steven M. Specht. Mizzentop Publishing. New York, NY.

Coiled Serpent: Poets Arising from the Cultural Quakes & Shifts of Los Angeles (2016) Collection of poems with other Los Angeles poets. Editors Neelanjana Banerjee, Daniel A. Olivas and Ruben J. Rodriguez

30 Poems in 30 Days: Writing Prompts & Poems from Tiferet Journal (2015) Poems with Lisa Sawyer, Monica Gurevich-Importico, Tracy Brooks, Kimberly Burnham, Udo Hintze, Shannon S. Hyde, Catriona Knapman, Maureen Kwiat Meshenberg, Louise Jayne Moriarty, Hazel Saville, Ambika Talwar, and Laura J. Wolfe. Creating Calm Network Publishing

A Single Drop of Blood (2015) with Gary D. Blankenship, Traci Siler, Keri Colestock, Ed Bremson, Ambika Talwar and 15 inspirational authors.

"Rishikesh: Silent Hum of Mystery" A biographical story in *Himalayan Bridge* (2015) with Editors Niraj Kumar, George

van Driem, P. Stobdan. K W Publishers Pvt. Ltd. New Delhi, India.

"Opening the Doorway of the Universe," "Open Palms," & *"A Prayer for All Time"* with Susan Rogers, Lois P. Jones, Maja Trochimczyk & others in *Meditation on Divine Names.* (2012) Edited by Maja Trochimczyk, Moonrise Press, Los Angeles, Ca.

4 Stars & 25 Roses: Poems for my Father by Ambika Talwar. (2011) Published by Golden Matrix Visions. Los Angeles, Ca.

"My One-Minute Waltz" & *"Waltzing with Chopin in a Foreign Land,"* with others in *Chopin with Cherries.* (2010) Edited by Maja Trochimczyk, Moonrise Press, Los Angeles, Ca.

"Endangered Species: Old Suitcases, Old Lovers," "Of My Becoming," "You, the World Inside Me!" & Other poems in *Inkwater Ink,* Vol. 3, (2008) Published by Inkwater Press, Portland, Or.

Creative Resonance: Poetry: Elegant Play, Elegant Change by Ambika Talwar (2006) Published by Golden Matrix Visions. Los Angeles, Ca.

"Naked Geometry" A poem in *So Luminous the Wildflowers – An Anthology of California Poets.* Edited by Paul Suntup (2003) Huntington Beach, Ca.

path
no path

sacred
(way)
home

Final Meditations
from... The Book of Wisdom

21.

ὅσα τέ ἐστιν κρυπτὰ καὶ ἐμφανῆ ἔγνων·ἡ γὰρ
πάντων τεχνῖτις ἐδίδαξέν με σοφία

I learned both what is secret and what is manifest,
for Sophia, the fashioner of all things,
taught me.

22.

Ἔστιν γὰρ ἐν αὐτῇ πνεῦμα νοερόν, ἅγιον,
μονογενές, πολυμερές, λεπτόν, εὐκίνητον,
τρανόν, ἀμόλυντον, σαφές, ἀπήμαντον,
φιλάγαθον, ὀξύ, ἀκώλυτον,

For in Her there is a spirit that is intelligent, holy,
unique, manifold, subtle, mobile, clear, unpolluted,
distinct, invulnerable, loving the good, keen,
irresistible,...

24.

πάσης γὰρ κινήσεως κινητικώτερον
σοφία,διήκει δὲ καὶ χωρεῖ διὰ πάντων διὰ τὴν
καθαρότητα·

For Sophia is more mobile than any motion;
because of Her pureness,
She pervades and penetrates all things.

(*The Book of Wisdom,* a book in the *Bible,* is scripture of the
Eastern Orthodox Church.)

(to be continued...)

Made in the USA
Columbia, SC
30 December 2020

30082061R00153